ENDORSEMENTS

The most important lesson in the book is that you don't have to be a national champion or an Olympian for these lessons to apply. They share important skills on leadership, determination, teamwork, and striving for excellence. I'm confident the lessons in this book will work for you, too.
- Earvin "Magic" Johnson

I got to know Lisa and Bridgette when I was an executive at SAP – they spoke at several of our key customer events. This book represents a passion I have witnessed first-hand from them, the "heart and mind of a coach". Just like a professional athlete needs a coach to guide them to their best performance, so does every great executive. Every great champion had a great coach with an exceptional playbook. This book gives you the playbook for success in highly competitive markets.
- Sanjay Poonen,
COO, VMware (formerly President, SAP)

T0150858

Sports and business offer useful parallels which From the Court to the Boardroom so nicely articulates. Executives and athletes, alike, climb to the top of their fields, using smart, strategic thinking to get and stay ahead of their competitors. Lisa Leslie and Bridgette Chambers have produced a well written, enjoyable business book that gets directly to the heart of getting ahead.

- Whitney Johnson

Thinkers50 and critically-acclaimed author of *Disrupt Yourself: Putting the Power of Disruptive Innovation to Work*

I coach the top 2% of executives and can tell you without a doubt, the marketplace is every bit as competitive as sports played in college or the ranks of the pros. Nurturing the skills and talents learned in sports and understanding how to translate that competitive energy into business success is a champion move only the top executives master.

- Dr. Betty Orlandino

Master Executive Coach & Author of *Fast Track to the Corner Office for Women*

From the Court to the Boardroom

FROM THE COURT TO THE BOARDROOM

Lisa Leslie and Bridgette Chambers

NEW YORK

NASHVILLE • MELBOURNE • VANCOUVER

FROM THE COURT TO THE BOARDROOM

The Path to Empowerment

Published in New York, New York, by Morgan James Publishing. Morgan James is a trademark of Morgan James, LLC. www.MorganJamesPublishing.com

The Morgan James Speakers Group can bring authors to your live event. For more information or to book an event visit The Morgan James Speakers Group at www.TheMorganJamesSpeakersGroup.com.

ISBN 9781683504184 paperback
ISBN 9781683504191 eBook
Library of Congress Control Number: 2017900868

Cover Design by:
Chris Treccani
www.3dogdesign.net

Interior Design by:
Chris Treccani
www.3dogdesign.net

In an effort to support local communities, raise awareness and funds, Morgan James Publishing donates a percentage of all book sales for the life of each book to Habitat for Humanity Peninsula and Greater Williamsburg.

Get involved today! Visit
www.MorganJamesBuilds.com

Our thanks to the following people for their incredible support and talents:

- Mason Smith, for phenomenal editing and shaping our voice into one.
- Ioana-Marin Rogojinaru, for exceptional cover art and illustrations.
- Monica Kressman, for creativity and photography
- Alicia Dunams, for helpful networking and marketing support.

I would like to dedicate this to my wonderful husband, Michael, who supports all of my endeavors! You lead me with love and push me to believe I can achieve my dreams! You support me, no matter the outcome! I'm so thankful God made you, just for me! I hope I inspire my children to strive to be the best they can be in all that they do! If you guys just do your best, I know you will end up at the top! Mommy loves you always! I would be silly not to mention my mom, who jump started the idea that I could be anything and do anything as long as I keep God first and remember the 7 P's: Proper, Prior, Preparation, Prevents, Piss, Poor, Performance! Thanks, Mom, you are truly the best mom and dad a girl could ask for! And last, but not least, thank you to Bridgette for being such an awesome inspiration and friend! I couldn't have picked a better person to team up with! Let's take over the world, Yang!

- **Lisa Leslie**

Like all of my endeavors, I dedicate them to my incredible family. Brenda, Matthew, and Michelle, you have provided me with the inspiration and fearlessness to achieve my dreams. I do my best work with you in my mind! Bren, thank you for believing in me, no matter the challenge.

Additionally, I'm thankful for the family and mentors in my life who left me with the lasting impression that anything is possible and nothing is out of reach. Of course, I must thank and recognize my dear friend and co- author, Lisa, for the personal, spiritual, and professional encouragement and motivation. Thanks, Ying, for joining forces once again to empower others and stir greatness in those who want to take their career to the next level and their life to new heights.

- Bridgette Chambers

FOREWORD

___

Earvin "Magic" Johnson

Success in athletics is a lot more than gaining strength, speed, agility, and the particular skills of basketball, football, soccer, or any other sport. Becoming a successful athlete means developing strong mental skills, too. These mental skills will help you every step of the way, for the rest of your life, in just about any profession you pursue. Lisa Leslie and Bridgette Chambers are great examples of having all the athletic abilities and the mental skills, too!

Having known Lisa since she was a star high school athlete to becoming one of the great women's basketball players dominating the court and leading her teams to California state basketball titles, NCAA crowns, WNBA championships, and Olympic gold medals, she is a long way from being finished. She took the focus, teamwork and drive for excellence that she learned as an athlete to become a successful role model, sports analyst, businesswoman, and motivational speaker. On top of all that, she has managed to be an amazing mom, a great wife, and a loving daughter.

Bridgette Chambers was also a great athlete, first as a swimmer and water polo player, and she later became a talented soccer player in school and in the U.S. Army. She used her mental discipline in the business world to become a well-known corporate turnaround expert and successful CEO of several huge corporations.

Lisa and Bridgette are both impressive women, but they are also really kind, caring people who want to share what they've learned and help others to achieve.

From the Court to the Boardroom describes what it was like for both of them as young girls realizing that they enjoyed competing in sports to success after their playing days. It explains how they applied those lessons to their business careers. The most important lesson in the book is that you don't have to be a national champion or an Olympian for these lessons to apply. They share important skills on leadership, determination, teamwork, and striving for excellence. I'm confident the lessons in this book will work for you, too.

- Earvin "Magic" Johnson

ABOUT THE AUTHORS

At every possible level of play, **Lisa Leslie** was the most dominant player in women's basketball. She led Morningside High School to two California state championships; at the University of Southern California, she was the Pac-10's all-time leader in points, rebounds, and block shots; she played on the United States' Olympic gold-medal-winning teams in 1996, 2000,  2004, and 2008; and, as a multiple MVP, she led the Los Angeles Sparks to back-to-back WNBA championships.

But Lisa is so much more than an athlete: she has been a model for the Wilhelmina Agency, the author of the memoir *Don't Let the Lipstick Fool You*, is currently a television sports analyst, a motivational speaker, an entrepreneur, founder of several non-profit organizations, and former co-owner of the L.A. Sparks.

As if this weren't enough, she and her husband, Michael Lockwood, are parents of Lauren and MJ.

Bridgette Chambers is an ABA award-winning CEO, turnaround and growth strategist, and author of *Profitable Problem Solving*™, the highly-acclaimed book that teaches entrepreneurs and business leaders strategies to ensure corporate profit and personal gain.

Chambers served as CEO of Constellation Research, a Silicon Valley-based research technology firm helping clients unleash the power of emerging and disruptive technologies. Then, as CEO of America's SAP Users Group (ASUG), Chambers led a transformation that doubled membership, enhanced service and delivery, and rebuilt the corporate culture. During her tenure, ASUG won two ABA awards, including Company of the Year, and ABA named Chambers its Maverick of the Year.

Chambers is co-founder of BGBC Marketing, dedicated to helping entrepreneurs and small business leaders grow their enterprises. She has also flexed her community evangelist brand by co-founding EmpoweredW, a global community of entrepreneurs, innovators, and thought leaders who share a passion for collective female success.

A celebrated keynote speaker on the topics of transformational leadership, innovation, and entrepreneurship, she has shared the stage with Colin Powell, Lisa Leslie, Seth Godin, Michael Eisner, and other notable personal brands.

TABLE OF CONTENTS

———

RE-IGNITE. RISE. REACH.

⎯⎯⎯

Chicago, Las Vegas, Orlando, New York ... which city are we in today?

Our Leadership 2.0 tour, the first of our many professional endeavors together, was ambitious.

Leadership 2.0 was the name for a series of leadership workshops we jointly facilitated, aimed at developing leadership skills for professionals managing large, complex projects. Leadership 2.0 delivered educational and inspirational content via workshops and online interactions. Eventually, 100,000 professionals would take part. Some participants would later tell us that they saw the two of us as an unlikely duo — yet by the time we kicked the program into gear, the feedback had changed to one of complete appreciation.

We traveled the globe and talked to standing-room-only crowds about strategies to improve and mature the leadership skills of businessmen and women. Our audiences were a healthy mix of early-career professionals and others who had held leadership positions for decades. The special brand of strategy we shared was one enveloped in the competitive foundation that we both sparked and nurtured as athletes. The message resonated with the audience every time.

We share a similar perspective on life, and we enjoyed every moment of it. Audience members could sense the way we enjoyed the opportunity to work together. After our time on stage at the Leadership 2.0 events, we heard feedback that was incredibly rewarding and uplifting, as people shared that our messages had given new enthusiasm, confidence, and direction to people striving to achieve more in their careers and accomplish more for their communities.

As businesswomen, we knew the feedback was pointing to an underserved opportunity to inspire, guide, lead, and pay-it-forward. This notion would become the basis of EmpoweredW, the global community we co-founded to support, nurture, and network with entrepreneurial and innovative women.

This notion also serves as the basis of this book.

In our minds, getting on each plane and stepping to the front of each stage was a chance to lead by example and give to others focused on becoming their best.

In *From the Court to the Boardroom*, we will share our perspectives on reaching your full potential, because success is subjective and every individual wants to be successful. We just want to make sure you have reached your full potential and empower you to do just that.

Before we ever took an MBA or PhD course or set foot in a business office, each of us spent thousands of hours practicing and playing sports. Our own experiences include Olympic and professional basketball, youth swimming, volleyball, softball, intensely competitive amateur soccer, and track and field.

We're willing to bet that you share that with us — that you, too, spent thousands of hours on the court, the field, the pool, the diamond, or the track.

What makes us so sure?

Fact 1: You picked up this book, which suggests you are serious about your business career.

Fact 2: An astonishing percentage of seriously successful businesspeople and entrepreneurs have backgrounds as athletes.

In fact, 97% percent of C-level (CEO, COO, CFO) women have athletic backgrounds, and 52% played a sport at their university. They include Hewlett-Packard CEO Meg Whitman, a former Princeton lacrosse and squash player; Gatorade and Stokely-Van Camp president and CEO Sue Wellington, who was captain of Yale's swim team; Spiegel Catalog CEO Melissa Payner, a former gymnast at Ohio State and Arizona State; and Betsy Bernard, CEO of AT&T's consumer business, who was a competitive ski racer. The competitive backgrounds of male CEOs range from professional tennis (Stephen R. Appleton, Micron Technology) to football (Jeffrey Immelt, General Electric, Dartmouth) to baseball (W. James McNerney Jr. Boeing, Yale) — not to mention the many thousands of executives and entrepreneurs who were high school or college (or Little League or Pop Warner) baseball pitchers and football linemen, tennis players, and track-and-field high jumpers.

So, our conclusion: you probably spent many, many hours honing your athletic skills (both physical and mental); you experienced everything from crushing defeat to glorious victory; and (best of all!) chances are you had the experience of learning from a talented, dedicated, focused coach who demonstrated, every single day, all of the life-affirming qualities of *leadership*.

We would love to sit down with each and every one of you over a glass of wine or cup of coffee to hear all your sports stories (we're sure they are thrilling, every single one of them!), but for the purposes of *From the Court to the Boardroom*, the specifics aren't important. It is our firm belief (and the basis of this book) that everyone who participates seriously in sports, no matter what the sport and no matter the level, learns principles that contribute to success not only in athletics, but also in business and in life.

Now, as you embark on your career as a budding entrepreneur or in a corporate environment, do you have the sense that those thousands of hours you gave to sports were just fun and games, a way you had of filling the empty hours while you waited to get started with your real life? Or, if you are a mid-career businessperson or entrepreneur, or even a late-career executive, picking up this book in hopes of reading something that will spark your enthusiasm to tackle the challenge ahead, do you imagine your athletic career was totally unrelated to your later business success?

Our emphatic reply: *No!* Absolutely not.

Whether or not you realize it, it's time to re-ignite! Those years as an athlete gave you what you need to be successful in your career today.

Consider this scenario:

The noise of the crowd has a frantic, anxious edge to it. Upbeat music blasts through the loudspeakers. Players on the bench are on their feet, waving their hands, pumping their fists, shouting encouragement.

A shot goes up, clanks off the rim, comes down into our center's hands.

"Time out! Time out!" cries our coach, waving for the officials' attention. The team gathers around the coach, starters crouching in a tight circle, surrounded by bench players who are huddled around, leaning in close so they don't miss a word. "What are the metrics?" asks the coach.

A glance up at the scoreboard. "Down by five," says a player. "Sixty seconds to play."

The coach looks around the circle, from one player to the next. "What are our strengths and qualities that make us winners?"

The center answers, "Relentless work ethic and our ability to persevere through tough times and rise to the occasion, Coach. When other people are clocking out at five on the dot, I stay until I've finished my project. Meeting my project deadline is a must. I always leave on a made basket. I always make sure I've polished my project to perfection. I do my speed drills, lift those weights, and practice my moves until muscle memory takes over." Yes I'm talking about practice. (Allen Iverson voice)

The point guard answers, "Game face, Coach. When I show up for work, no one's in any doubt that I'm there to reach my goals: I'm concentrating on meeting my benchmarks, exceeding my goals, getting better and better at my job, and leading by example. Playing my role on the court and always maintaining my professionalism."

The small forward says, "Competitive drive, Coach. I'm focused on institutional goals—improving the brand, delivering the best product at the best price, enhancing shareholder value — and I'm focused on my own personal goals and the team's goals, too. I'm driven to achieve!"

The power forward chimes in, "Sharing the glory, Coach. I'm plenty confident, but I'm not too proud to give my teammates credit! I know I'm only going to be as successful as my colleagues. We're a team!"

The coach says, "We need to play smart and aggressive without fouling. No cheap shots. You all deserve to be here because you put in the hard work, right?"

The shooting guard says, "Right, Coach, totally aggressive—but within the rules! Breaking laws and company policies always costs more than it's worth. I'm not afraid to push and shove. That's part of the game. But getting ejected from the game just hurts the team."

"Who knows our institutional goal?" asks the coach.

One of the bench players says, "To outwork the competition, work together as one unit, and WIN!"

The coach and the players give a cheer.

Reminded of what it's all about, the team sprints onto the court, plays suffocating defense, grabs two tough rebounds, puts down a couple of three- pointers, and wins the game — achieving its institutional goal!

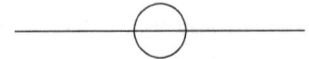

Ridiculous, right?

You may be asking, *Who plays hoops like that? What do all these business-world concepts have to do with basketball?*

Well, we believe business has *everything* to do with basketball, soccer, baseball, water polo, or whatever sport you played as a kid, a high schooler, a collegian, or even a professional. The impact of the principles you learned as a young athlete extends far, far beyond the court, the field, and the pool.

Viewed from the outside, winning a match and achieving success in business may look totally different from each other. Participants in the two endeavors wear different uniforms, have different ways of keeping score, listen to different buzzers, and play by radically different rules—but they have more in common than most people believe. Successful athletics and successful business practice share an underlying set of basic principles.

In our thousands of hours of practice and competition, we absorbed these principles into the very fibers of our being.

You did, too, didn't you?

Were you a club gymnast, a high school miler, a college football player, or any other sort of athlete? Did you go pro and play at the highest level your sport has to offer? Did you have one of the great experiences any young person can have: to play under the mentorship of a great coach?

If you are one of the fortunate women or men who can answer *Yes* to those questions, then those principles are still part of you — maybe buried deep, maybe barely recollected, but definitely still there — ready to serve you incredibly well in your life, in your personal and working relationships, and, especially, in your business career.

These principles are in you, possibly at a below-conscious level, just waiting to be identified, recognized, revived, sharpened, and put to new uses.

Those principles are what *From the Court to the Boardroom* is all about.

In this book, we have three goals. We call them our Three *R*s.

1. We encourage you to RE-IGNITE the passion, intensity, and focus you knew in your athletic years.
2. We encourage you to RISE to meet the challenges of a successful business career.
3. We encourage you to REACH beyond your own accomplishments in order to have a broad, widening, positive impact.

Let's begin by taking a step back to your childhood and looking at what happened when you began to compete (we know what you went through, because we went through it, too).

You gained a sense of who you really are.

You learned to listen to your coach, fulfill your role on the team, and work together with your teammates.

You discovered that winning is a lot more satisfying than just getting by.

You learned how rotten it feels to lose, but then you learned that losing isn't the end of the world. You learned to make something positive out of it. You learned to practice harder and smarter and come back from defeat.

You learned how satisfying it is to share the entire gamut of competition, winning and losing, with your teammates.

You began to ask yourself, for the very first time in your life, whether you truly wanted to be successful.

Once you pictured yourself as a champion, you asked yourself, "What's it going to take?" You came to realize that success requires more than just jogging up and down a sunlit soccer field. It takes hard work.

Some kids decide, *I enjoy jogging around in the sun and giving the ball a kick whenever it comes to me. Winning is nice, but it isn't worth the sweat. After all, even if the team never wins a game, we still get a pizza party at the end of the season.*

But other kids get a taste of winning and decide, *I really like this feeling. I really, really want to win. If winning is going to take 10,000 hours of hard, hard work, then how soon can we get started?*

You were one of those kids, weren't you?

If you weren't one of those kids—if you never worked with a talented coach, if you never made the decision to put in those 10,000 hours of practice, if you never tasted victory, if you never experienced how good it feels to come back from defeat … we don't believe you would be reading this book.

When you decided not just to play, but to win … when you committed to the **purpose** of being a winner … you discovered the talent and the reservoirs of strength you had inside yourself.

But you soon realized you couldn't just decide to win, couldn't glide by on talent alone, and simply playing the game wasn't enough to make your natural-born talent blossom to its fullest. Sweating and huffing and puffing wasn't enough, and becoming a winner wasn't just a matter of getting faster and stronger. You needed to play smarter, too. You needed the **discipline** to listen, to learn, to practice, to focus, to hone your skills, to read your opponents, to become a student of the game.

Surely that was enough to make you into a winner, wasn't it? Well, no, the winner brings one more thing.

She *brings it!*

When it was time to practice, you brought a **competitive drive** that sharpened your skills to a razor's edge and pulled your teammates along with you. And, when it was game-time, you cranked that already-revving competitive drive into another gear. You focused. You competed. You either won or you left the field after the last buzzer, covered in sweat, aching, breathing hard, and holding your head up because you knew you'd given it everything you had.

In organized athletics, we identified our purpose, we achieved discipline, and we brought our competitive drive. We learned to compete to win, to overcome adversity, to take risks, to play with passion, and to work with a team.

And if you stick with it, you also learned to be driven, focused, deliberate, determined, collaborative, inspired, motivated, resolved, self-assured, competitive, entrepreneurial, and accomplished.

Aren't these exactly the skills anyone needs to succeed in the business world?

If you are able to **re-ignite** these qualities, you'll **rise** in whatever business or entrepreneurial arena you choose to compete in. And as you rise, you'll discover how satisfying it is to **reach** farther and wider, extending your impact in incredible ways.

High-level executives and successful entrepreneurs report that their athletic backgrounds have helped them advance their careers in many ways, but when they are asked to condense it to a single factor, they consistently say, *"Athletics taught me leadership."*

The luckiest athletes had the opportunity to learn from a coach with well-developed leadership skills. Consider what a dedicated coach does. She brings together a disparate group of athletes, teaches them essential skills, gives them focus, molds them into a cohesive team, outlines a winning strategy, and helps them adjust to changing circumstances.

Whether it's on the basketball court or in the corporate boardroom, leaders move us forward. They provide confidence, enthusiasm, and discipline. Leadership is bold, yet vulnerable. It is simultaneously complex and simple. It happens in the sideline with a whistle and in a staff meeting. But it isn't something that happens only in these formal settings. It's something that happens 24 hours a day, 7 days a week. It happens in what a leader says, what she does, how she behaves, how she reacts to varying circumstances, and how she lives her life. In our sports careers, we learned that leadership is something that leaders live.

In our careers as athletes (and even across a backgammon board, competing with our mothers!), we learned six key principles that made us winners on the basketball court and the soccer field. These same six principles, translated to the corporate arena, have consistently led us to business success.

But this book is not about us. It's about *you!*

We are convinced that our athletic experience — and yours, too — have provided all of us with a common foundation. As you read the principles and insights we've gathered in our sports careers and how we've applied them to our business lives, we hope you will be reminded of your own sports career, realize how you learned these principles and brought them to the playing field, and recognize ways they can contribute to your own corporate success.

Our six principles are:

1. **Lead by Example.** Leadership is a full-time job, there are no shortcuts, and you must be authentic.
2. **Rediscover the Heart of a Champion.** Have the heart to dig down deep, the relentless work ethic that walks the walk, and the self-motivation to outwork your competition.
3. **Have a Winning Attitude.** Observe the Three *F*s: be FIRM, be FRIENDLY, and be FAIR.
4. **Share the Glory.** Appreciate the contributions of all your teammates, treat everyone with respect, and never get *too big for your britches*.
5. **Perseverance.** In tough times, who are you? Stay positive, set and achieve incremental goals, and learn from your failures.
6. **Empower Through Leadership.** As a leader — whether you're a coach, a CEO, or the president of the United States — your ultimate responsibility is to build a team of leaders. Mentor your colleagues. Volunteer. Be *of service* to others.

In this book, we will explore what these principles have meant to us in our athletic and business careers. But this isn't just a stroll down memory lane. This book is meant to be a call-to-action for those of you who have that winning foundation but may need a little reminder of how to engage that part of yourself in your career. Re-igniting this foundation has the power to propel you past any career plateau or transformation you may be experiencing.

Remember what it felt like to be an athlete: the surge of adrenaline, the camaraderie, the thrill of competition, the satisfaction of striving against the odds, the incomparable exhilaration of winning.

Now ask yourself: Have I replicated that in my professional career? If not, what are you waiting for?

At various stages in our business careers, we have benefited immeasurably from the competitive advantage that our foundation in competitive sports created for us.

We've made use of the six principles to succeed during the good times.

Whenever we've experienced really tough times, when nothing seemed to be going our way, we've used these principles to **re-ignite**, **rise**, and **reach**.

We believe you can, too.

Your foundation in competitive sports is a remarkable, unbeatable competitive advantage. Wherever you started — whether it's on the basketball court or the running track or some other competitive endeavor—we hope to rekindle the excitement of competition and fuel your career trajectory or entrepreneurial goals.

We invite you to join us on our journey *From the Court to the Boardroom*.

CHAPTER ONE

Lead by Example

True leadership — whether it takes place on the court or the field, in the locker room, in the office, or in the boardroom—is thoughtful, disciplined, confident, and, most of all, *authentic*.

Genuine, effective leadership, the sort of leadership with the power to carry you to success, is much more than a skill you pull out of your toolbox as needed, then keep locked away the rest of the time.

Leadership is not something you *do*. It's something you *live, and it's something you give.*

There are no shortcuts to leadership, because someone is always watching.

Let's start our discussion of leadership at the logical place: the making of a leader.

Learning to lead a group started with our very first coach.

Think back, if you can, to the first day of your very first team meeting. You and your new teammates were excited, jabbering, full of energy. Whatever the sport, you probably didn't consider yourself a rank amateur. Maybe you'd played a lot of hoops on the asphalt court in your neighborhood. You'd tossed the baseball around with your dad or your mom or your big brothers and sisters. You'd kicked a soccer ball around at the local park. You were good at this! You were a natural! You were ready to play!

What did your new coach do? He or she stood there in the midst of that frantic mayhem, clapped her hands, blew her whistle, and said, "Listen up, everyone!"

Listen up?

Just like every other adult in your life, she wanted from you the one thing you didn't want to give her—maybe the one thing you *couldn't* give.

She wanted you to settle down. To fall quiet. To sit still. To listen.

At the time, you didn't know that was more than just a grownup's typically unreasonable demand. It was your first lesson in leadership.

The first, and by far the most important, part of becoming a leader might have seemed like the exact opposite of leading.

Shut up and listen.

You might ask, *How can I lead anyone with my mouth shut?*

None of us walks onto the basketball court or the soccer field the first time knowing all the mechanics of the sport. Likewise, no matter how excellent our preparation—our MBA, our past entrepreneurial endeavors, our previous professional experience— none of us walks into any new job or market knowing it all. There's always a learning curve.

The same can be said about leadership, too. Leadership isn't just a matter of gaining competence at your job, getting promoted into a position with a "leadership" title, and handing out orders. Leadership has its own mechanics, and none of us comes by them naturally. They must be learned.

Now, try to remember the first time she showed you how to hold the ball, adjusted the position of your elbow as you made a shot, showed you how to plant your foot on a soccer kick, corrected your freestyle stroke, or placed your hands correctly on a baseball bat. A lot of kids — you were one of them, weren't you? —considered themselves the king of the neighborhood basketball court or the queen of the soccer field.

Recall how your coach patiently insisted that you try the skill her way. You didn't quite get what she meant. You already knew how to do this, didn't you?

But you decided to try it her way, just once, to prove her wrong.

Remember how the ball arced high through the air and fell so cleanly through the hoop?

Remember how the soccer ball left your kicking foot with that solid, satisfying *thump!* and curled into the corner of the net?

Okay, so maybe your first try wasn't quite that successful. But little by little, you came to understand what she was trying to show you. First, you understood it with your brain; then your body started to catch on; and then, gradually, it became part of your muscle memory. It felt really good, didn't it? We'll bet you remember— or *seem* to remember — something pretty close to that.

Even more than the mechanical skill, you remember realizing that this man or woman knew a lot more than you did about the sport.

You remember your early excitement at how this adult — your first coach! — was willing and eager to share her knowledge with you.

You started hanging on your coach's every word. You listened!

We'll bet you remember the unfamiliar feeling of gaining respect for your coach, gradually coming to put your trust in her, wanting to perform for her, wanting to prove you'd been listening.

That was when you began to learn not just to follow, but to lead.

I remember very well the day I became a good listener.

I was in eighth grade. My school didn't have a team, but I was on a club, and I'd just won my first trophy. Oh, yeah, I knew how to play.

So, my only male cousin, who was 18, offered to take me to a gym. He promised to help me get better.

When we got to the gym on the first day, I was ready to play, but the first thing he said was, "Put down the ball and give me ten pushups."

What? I just wanted to play some hoops.

But he told me, "Listen, this can be our first day or our last day. It's up to you. You can decide you want to be the best, and you can start listening. Or, you can decide it just isn't worth it to you."

This was just my second year, and I had realized I was way behind the competition. I was playing against girls who'd been on teams since they were five or six years old.

So I decided, right there and then, to listen. That's when I became a student of the game.

I did those pushups, and all these years later, I know those pushups (and all the millions of pushups I've done since) are just as much part of being a champion as learning to dunk.

I'm grateful for all the basketball my cousin taught me, but I'm equally thankful for him teaching me to listen.

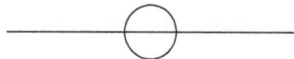

We could make a list a thousand items long of the skill-specific lessons we learned along the way: how to set a pick, how to juke a defender, how to blast off the block in a swimming race, how to slide into home, how to get into prime physical condition, how to get faster and quicker. But only after we absorbed that first lesson — *Shut up and listen!* — could all of the coach's other lessons start to take hold.

You admired your coach's technical knowledge of your sport and her skill at sharing it with you and your teammates. But eventually you discovered that your coach was more than a one-dimensional person. You may have overheard your parents saying something about your age-group coach: *She's so thoughtful; she gives of her time so freely.* You may have witnessed your coach around the halls of your high school, in earnest discussion with other students or teachers. Or, during a game, you may have seen your coach display a depth of character that impressed you.

I was lucky enough to have a grandfather who coached for over 50 years. For his entire adult life, he coached every sport that came along: football, basketball, baseball. You name it.

There weren't many girls' teams back then, so I played on every team he had. My grandfather had me tuck my hair up in my hat so I didn't look quite so much like a girl.

He challenged me more than any coach I would ever play for. He had a way of reaching that fire inside my soul and making it roar.

In a huddle, in the dugout, before a game, at halftime, he would walk us through exactly what we needed to do in order to take advantage of our talents, play our best, and finish the game as winners.

One thing I learned from him, on top of listening, was that everyone has a particular role to play on the team. If you're the clutch player with the ability to score some points, then you're the one we need to get the ball to; but just because you may not be the clutch player, that doesn't mean you're not an important part of the team. Everyone needs to learn where they fit in, how they can contribute, and how they can all come together to accomplish their goal.

He taught every child he coached, and showed us by his example, what it means to be a smart leader and a good citizen. I truly believe that my grandfather's example resonates in all the generations of leaders he influenced and nurtured. Those kids went on to mature into adults and serve our country, serve our corporations, and serve our communities.

I know he resonates in me.

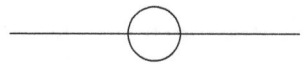

But your coach wasn't the only leader you came into contact with in athletics. You probably learned a lot from your teammates, too.

Do you remember the first time you took notice of a teammate's fierce attitude on the court or the field?

If you were on your high school's cross country running team, the beginning of every practice was pleasant, but gradually, as you covered the miles, ran those track intervals, or sprinted those hill-climbs, it got to be work. Your lungs wanted to burst, your legs screamed in pain, and you felt the overpowering urge to ease off. But there was one runner on the team who always attacked the last hill-climb just as hard as the first one. *She must be some kind of aerobic beast,* you thought. But at the end of the workout, you saw her gasping for breath, and you realized she was no natural aerobic monster. She wasn't even in much better condition than you. She simply wanted it more than you. She intended to be the best.

Or you might have practiced with a basketball player who had a smooth move to the hoop that you couldn't defend. *A natural,* you thought. But when the coach blew the whistle to end practice, this player stayed on the court, practicing and practicing to improve what you'd thought was a perfect, natural move.

Then, you may have gotten to know this teammate away from the field. Chances are, she was the sort of student who studied hard, never missed an assignment, made the absolute most of her natural intelligence, and earned excellent grades. In her spare time, she may have volunteered at a local nursing home or animal shelter.

She probably would have laughed if you'd told her she was a leader. But she *lived* leadership in everything she did. Without even being aware of it, she *gave* to everyone around her.

You learned all sorts of things from your coach, from your teammates, and even from your opponents. You learned to accept the leadership of others, and little by little, as your skills (both physical and mental) improved—as you earned it—you probably discovered that your teammates started watching you for mechanics, for strategy, for conditioning tips, for flexibility drills, and even for inspiration. Without opening your mouth, you became a leader.

You might have found yourself elected team captain. Or, without the official title, you might have found other teammates coming to you for advice.

Now, it finally became time to open your mouth.

If I saw a player who was really good at a particular skill, I might pull her aside and say, "Hey, when you have a moment, maybe you could show me how to do that shot." That way, I not only might add another tool to my repertoire, but it's also an awesome thing to do to build camaraderie.

And if I saw someone doing something that wasn't working, I'd go over and offer to spend a little time sharpening her skill or getting her back on track by saying, "Let's meet before or after practice to get in some extra shots."

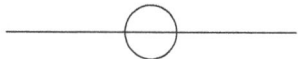

Leaders lead through word and deed, they lead by example, and they lead by demonstrating, in everything they do, that they don't expect anything to come easily. Especially, a leader never takes advantage of an unethical, sleazy, or cheap shortcut to success.

When I was growing in my career, I worked for a company that will remain nameless, and for people who will remain nameless.

I genuinely respected the guy I reported to, an executive member of the company and a member of the thought-management team. A serious dip in the economy was right around the corner, and he had the impressive financial competency to forecast the downturn. I had turned around several groups within the company, and they were turning some incredible numbers. I'd been introduced to the board, received several promotions, and was really thriving. Things were going great!

Among the many things I was dealing with, I had discovered some ongoing reporting errors. After a lot of sleuthing, I found the missing money. A computer script, designed to capture weekly revenue from products that we re-engineered and sold, was only capturing sales from Thursdays and Fridays. The sales from the rest of the week were missing. It was definitely a screw-up, but it wasn't intentional.

It had taken me three quarters to get my arms around the problem and solve it. By the time I figured it out, our figures were showing $1 million less in revenue than they should have.

Right in the late part of Q3, while we were budgeting and planning for the next season, I went to my supervisor with the information.

"Congratulations," he told me. "I'm glad you found it, but don't put it in your budget. I'm going to claim that I'm going to grow revenues starting from the basis I have. That will give us a great head-start on maintaining revenues in the downturn."

I objected: "What do you mean? I can't not report this million dollars. I signed the Sarbanes-Oxley forms, committing to reporting things properly. You want me to go in and lie, so I can sandbag a million bucks? You want me to be dishonest so we can get bigger bonuses?"

Long story short: He told me if I reported this million dollars honestly—if I made it a reporting issue to get corrected in the previous fiscal year—then I shouldn't expect to remain part of the team.

"What do you mean, not part of the team?"

"You won't be a trusted member of the team," he said.

Really? I thought. This is how it works? I've busted my ass to get to this position, and this is the kind of decision you expect me to make?

I still couldn't quite believe that I understood what he was saying correctly. He was such a smart guy; he could have thrived by persevering within the rules. But his plan — apparently, his character — was to take the easy shortcut. I still didn't quite know what he meant. Would my reputation suffer? Was I going to be fired?

I have to admit, I really had to give this a lot of thought. After all, I had a growing reputation and a family to support. It was really scary, because I didn't know what I would do if I lost this position.

I prayed about it, and I spent a lot of sleepless nights.

And then I went in to work and gave him the report, including the "lost" million dollars.

We worked out a package, and I left the company — not completely by my own choice.

But I'm actually very grateful things worked out like they did, because as one door closes, another always opens. When you make the right decisions, you truly tend to stay on the right path. I wouldn't be where I am now if that next door hadn't opened up for me.

Looking back on that situation, I can't help but be reminded of times when my soccer coach would tell us, "I want a mile." She would send us out on a crazy multi-mile rat race, up and down the bleachers, out around cones where she couldn't see us, and some of my teammates would cut corners. Even then, even while I saw my teammates cheating, it never occurred to me not to run the entire rat race. I knew I wouldn't get the full conditioning benefit by running half the course — and I knew I wouldn't be able to look myself in the mirror if I cheated.

Different arenas, but the same message: You never gain by cutting corners.

Our games and sports, our work lives, and every other aspect of our existence are constrained by rules, ordinances, policies, and laws.

What a pain in the neck — right? Why can't I just do what I want?

Because, if everyone did just what they were moved to do, society would grind to a halt.

Are we, maybe, overstating the case, just a little?

Not at all.

Think about the universal law that says, *Stop at a red light.* When was the last time you gave that even a moment's thought? Picture yourself in noon traffic, late for a meeting, losing a precious 60 seconds at a red light. Do you consider running it? Of course not, because you know there are consequences for breaking that rule, and because you understand that without that rule (and all the other basic rules of the road), none of us would have the freedom to get in our cars and drive.

Athletic contests are constrained by rules, too. If cross country runners start cutting corners during a race, the competition is going to collapse. If soccer players attack the goal as if the offside rule didn't exist, we might as well walk away from the field. The rules of the game provide the parameters within which we have the freedom to perform.

In its dependence on rules, policies, customs, and laws, business is no different from driving and competing. Our "free enterprise system" is only free because of the constraints imposed by corporation law, banking law, contract law, tax law, consumer protection law, and all the rest.

Does all of that regulation seem excessive? Does it sometimes seem like it exists for no purpose other than to employ armies of lawyers?

Well, we could argue the details of business law all day long and right into tomorrow — but our point is this: Business law exists for the purpose of leveling the "playing field," assuring all players that their competition won't be cheating, giving us dependable recourse if others try to cut corners, and liberating corporations and entrepreneurs to conduct their business.

The crucial difference between rules of the game and rules of business, we would argue, is that there's a referee on the basketball court and an umpire behind home plate. With the crowd cheering you on and the official watching to tell you when you stepped over the line, you had all the freedom in the world to play with aggression.

In business, on the other hand, you have no one constantly looking over your shoulder. As a result, businesspeople cheat far more than they ever cheated on the playing field.

The consequences of getting caught cheating in business (loss of reputation, loss of your job, and in the worst cases, even a prison sentence) are more severe than the consequences of committing a foul in basketball. But the rewards of cheating in business are often such that there will always be certain individuals willing to take the risk of breaking the law. Their attitude may be something like: *Those rules are fine for the "little people," but not for me!*

Then there are other people who learned the value of a level playing field on the basketball court, the water polo pool, and the soccer field — people like us who compete aggressively in business, but always within the rules. Rules make complete sense to us. Rules create order. Rules create transparency, which gives everyone the confidence to participate in the business system, invest, contribute, and innovate.

We believe rules give us the freedom to succeed.

We believe there is no reward, salary, or bonus worth the cost of our integrity. Following the rules, while still competing aggressively, allows us to walk away at the end of the day with our heads held high.

Being a leader takes fortitude, thoughtfulness, confidence, a really thick skin, and, most of all, *authenticity.*

A leader values the opinions of her colleagues, and she understands that different situations demand different approaches. Sometimes leadership means saying to the team, "Hey, guys, I really don't know how to do this. Any ideas? Do you have the solution?"

Some "leaders" operate on the theory that leadership means never having to admit that you don't know the answer to every question (and, yes, we used those apology-quotes around "leaders" intentionally, since we don't consider that type to be genuine leaders).

Leaders who won't admit to not knowing every answer are doomed to failure. They will always be functioning on the basis of incomplete information. They are struggling with one hand — or both hands — tied behind their backs.

But leadership does not mean being afraid to move until you've achieved consensus. When the leader is convinced that she's gathered, understood, and assimilated, every bit of relevant data, when she's considered various strategies, and when she's convinced she knows the right direction to proceed, then she isn't afraid to say, "You may not agree, but this is the way we're going to do it."

Putting a plan in place and getting started is essential to institutional success.

As Vince Lombardi said, "Plan your work, work your plan."

As Joel Ross and Michael Kami have written, "Without a strategy, an organization is like a ship without a rudder, going around in circles." And when Alice asked the Cheshire Cat, "Would you please tell me which way to go from here?" the Cat (that excellent business strategist) answered, "That depends a good deal on where you want to get to."

Since it's essential to get a plan in place, and since seeking perfect consensus (also known as "making everybody happy") is a fine prescription for keeping an organization muddling along without a rudder, the genuine leader understands when it's time to say, *You may not agree, but …*

Listening to a lengthy introduction, I stood just off-stage— gratuitous, since everyone in the audience knew exactly who I was — waiting for my cue to walk out and face 5,000 angry customers and volunteers.

I was the new CEO of an enormous trade association, tasked with the complete transformation of an organization on which these people utterly depended, and what I'd learned as I researched the association's situation and surveyed these stakeholders had astonished me. Their relationship to the association was not just a matter of business dealings; it was visceral and personal. When I'd asked them for a comparison, they had compared their relationship with the association to their relationship with their church.

The organization I was tasked with transforming was a trade association that provided advocacy and education to enterprise software users and experts — but my new stakeholders viewed it in quasi-religious terms. Many of them were customers, but a lot of them were dedicated, unpaid volunteers. They were as passionate about the association as they were about their spiritual lives.

The organization had been floundering, and the stakeholders' level of frustration was beyond belief — but they were also extremely wary of change in an organization that meant so much to them.

"Oh, my God," I realized, "these people are on fire." Waiting offstage, I could hear the tension in their whispering and rustling. "They are hugely pissed off."

Then I heard my name and the notes of a dramatic fanfare, my cue to stride out there and tell these 5,000 zealots that the association needed change—and not just change, but unpopular change—if it was to survive and thrive.

I reached the microphone and began, "You've just heard me referred to as 'chief executive.' Well, for the next hour and a half, I have a new title. Today, I invite you to think of me as 'she who can't please everyone.'"

I started my talk with a vision for the future. I asked for their support, enlisted their commitment, and made it clear that I was in no doubt that this transformation was going to change the association's relationship with its customers and volunteers.

I had known that changing things was going to be unpopular. As I spoke, I could hear murmurs of displeasure.

But I had also known that if I sought consensus, nothing would ever get done.

So, as I rolled out the new plan, I made it very clear: This plan is not open for debate.

I have discovered that most people, once they realize that your vision is sound and your respect for your audience is solid, will get on board. They may grumble, they may drag their heels a little bit, but before long, they'll follow you.

That was the case in this particular situation. My strategy wasn't popular, but the level of adoption, once I'd thoroughly made my case, was quite high. With the support of the 5,000 stakeholders in that room, we eventually doubled our membership, enhanced service and delivery, rebuilt the corporate culture, and created substantial growth in earnings.

Now, when I'm coaching people to feel okay with the fact that they're going to disappoint people, I use that story as a metaphor.

You have two choices: Spend your time arguing about the why of the situation or focus on the what.

By telling my audience "This is the plan," I was able to move them forward rapidly into a state of commitment, collaboration, and success.

Chalk Talk
- Chapter 1 -

* LEADERSHIP MUST
  BE LIVED 24/7

* NO SHORTCUTS

* AUTHENTICITY

CHAPTER TWO

——

The Heart of a Champion

(going from good to great)

I't's easy to lead when times are good, but can you be a great leader in tough times or times of change and uncertainty? Do you have it in you to dig down deep? Does your relentless work ethic drive you on to do what you must, not just what comes easy? It's up to you to set the bar: how high will you set it?

We see people all the time who just don't do well when they find themselves in a corporate culture that is predicated on the competitive spirit. We see them shy away from that and self-select to less competitive environments.

But, of course, there are others with the heart of the champion. They consistently work harder and accomplish more than anyone expects. They thrive on adversity and rise to meet every challenge.

What are you made of? Who are you in the moment? Did your athletic career teach you to dig down deep?

Do you possess the relentless work ethic that drives you to do what you must, rather than whatever comes easily?

When you feel yourself flagging, easing off, wanting to go home early or take a day off — and it's true, all of us feel that way, some of us more often than others — what happens? Do you get a sudden mental image of the competition practicing while you treat yourself to a vacation day? Do you picture them burning the midnight oil while you go home early?

Have you transferred the champion's heart that drove you to athletic success into your business career?

There's an old saying that goes: "If it doesn't bite as a pup, it won't bite as a dog."

That is, if it wasn't nurtured in you as a child (or a young athlete), it isn't likely to suddenly manifest itself in you, as if by magic, as an adult.

But we believe you can turn that old saying on its head. "If it bit as a pup, it can still bite as a dog."

Every one of us has a heart (a physical, pumping heart, sure, but also the kind that expresses itself through competitive drive). Those of us who had experience competing in sports got to feel that metaphorical heart pounding with the excitement of competing, trying, fighting, struggling, and winning. We know what it feels like, and even if we've never made the connection in our minds between the way our heart beats in an athletic contest and the way we drive ourselves to meet the challenges in our career, it's still the same. It's still there. It'll still bite. It just may need to be reawakened.

When you have that competitive fire inside you, it doesn't really matter if the task is silly or serious. It doesn't matter if it's a Little League baseball game or a high-stakes merger between two multi-billion-dollar corporations. A challenge presents itself, and somewhere deep in your cortex, synapses start firing, adrenalin starts flowing, and you're in the game. It's simply how your thought processes operate.

We've spent a lot of time, the two of us, discussing where that competitive fire comes from. Is it embedded in our DNA, inherited from past generations of competitors? Something we acquired as a result of our upbringing? Or is it a combination of both?

We enjoy arguing about it. We're competitive people, after all, and beating each other in an argument would be great! But the truth is, we don't have a clue whether the source of that competitive fire is to be found in nature or in nurture.

What we do know is that it starts really young.

I remember playing backgammon with my mother. "Okay, let's play one more," I remember telling my mom, "and this time, don't let me win." Then, when I won, I would get up and do my I Won I Won I Won dance, and I would feel so, so good.

As an adult, I've played Chutes and Ladders with my five-year-old niece. My niece goes racing ahead, teasing and trash talking and having a great time, so close to winning she can taste it. Then she pulls the card that sends her all the way back to the beginning. Hurt to the core, she bursts into tears. Here she is, just five years old, and she's got that competitive fire.

I play chess with my own children, and I have to laugh at the way my kids have picked up the same trash talking — during a game of chess, no less! — that I saw among my own parents and aunts and uncles. I recall the grownups playing cards or dominos, slapping the table, shouting, teasing, boasting, talking trash, and having such a good time competing with each other.

Competition is part of life. We compete on the basketball court and the soccer field, we compete for grades in school, we compete to get into college, we compete when we get there, and we compete on the job for the rest of our adult lives. Companies compete against each other. Brands compete for market share. Politicians compete for votes.

It's the foundation of so much of life; how could it not be a good thing to be good at competing? Why shouldn't we enjoy it?

We don't know precisely where the competitive drive comes from— nature or nurture — but we are convinced that competing at a young age can serve to harness and teach the drive.

That's how we learn that we're going to need to dig down really deep inside ourselves, practice harder and smarter, and truly give ourselves to the task, if we're going to be winners.

As young athletes, the inspiration was always right there in front of us: winning the next game, winning the next championship, taking home the trophy.

Eventually, digging down so deep becomes natural. We can't imagine doing things any differently. It becomes a sort of muscle memory.

And we see evidence all the time, in our own careers and in the careers of our colleagues, that the positive effects last a lifetime.

Sometimes we may need to seek out the inspiration that drives us to success ... and sometimes it seeks us out.

In the 1994 FIBA Women's World Championship, held in Sydney, Australia, we were beaten by Brazil in the semi-final round.

This wasn't supposed to happen. We were America, after all. We invented the game, for goodness sake. And this wasn't even the championship game. They'd taken us down in the semi-finals, so we were going to have to play Australia for a bronze medal.

As if to rub salt in our wounds, we had to share a bus from the arena to the hotel with the Brazilian team.

We were sitting on the right side of the bus, totally dejected, while the Brazilians, sitting across from us on the left side of the bus, were having a typical Brazilian celebration: music, dancing, shouting, laughing, and they were shaving their coach's head.

That's right. While we sat there in misery, they shaved their coach's head. Apparently, he had bet his players that they couldn't beat the Americans.

If they did, they could shave his head.

While the Brazilians were right there across the aisle, throwing the celebration that we were all convinced should have been ours, I felt so awful. But out of the awfulness came another emotion: absolute determination to work relentlessly, to play with all my heart, so I would never have to feel like that again. I promised myself, "We will never lose to another team. Especially not Brazil. From now on, it's all gold medals."

I wasn't the only one having this thought. My teammates were all high-level athletes, intensely competitive people. They were having the same thought.

While the Brazilians celebrated their triumph, they should have been thinking, Uh-oh, what have we done? We've awakened the beast. We've lit the fire in the Americans' hearts.

It takes some sort of inspiration to get the adrenaline flowing. Sometimes we have to seek out the inspiration, but sometimes it finds us. Sitting in misery during the Brazilians' celebration, we didn't have to seek inspiration. It was right there in our faces.

After that defeat in 1994, the USA women's basketball teams were virtually unstoppable, earning five Olympic gold medals in a row.

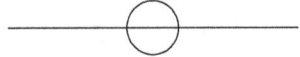

We've all heard the stories about the grandmother whose grandkid is trapped in the car that's about to roll over a cliff. The adrenaline flows, and she drags the car away from the edge of the cliff.

If you haven't heard that exact story, you've heard stories like it. And, as improbable as that story might be, we believe it's true. Why do we believe it? Because we all have an implicit belief that we have it in us to do impossible things to save our own loved ones.

Inspiration is all around us. Heart is in all of us.

Sometimes we apply it to a game, sometimes to our business, sometimes to our family, and sometimes to a worthwhile cause. But we know it's lurking there (harnessed and nurtured by our early sports experiences), just waiting for the challenge that sets us on fire, waiting for the inspiration to put us into overdrive.

We know a woman who has devoted her life to saving girls from sex trafficking. It's an amazing cause, but what can any of us do about it?

Well, this woman travels around from truck stop to truck stop, knocking on the doors of huge 18-wheelers and passing out leaflets.

She's a tiny little thing. It's a wonder she doesn't get mistaken for a road cone and is run over in those places.

But you know what? She's fearless, determined, and unstoppable because she's got so much heart. She's driven by her inspiration, and she digs down so deep.

It's been said that 10% of any game (or 10% or any business challenge) is the knowledge you bring to the problem.

That 10% is the easy part. The coach's first responsibility is to teach the skills; the corporation's responsibility is to recruit and hire employees with the education, general experience, and specific competency to do their jobs.

The difficult part is — wouldn't you know it? — the remaining 90%.

The remaining 90% is heart. Fight. Drive. Desire. The mental toughness that makes you dig deep.

When I was ten years old, I was by far the youngest and smallest girl on my water polo team. I lacked the size and strength of the other girls, and while I didn't show it, I knew I wasn't going to out-muscle anyone.

But I just wouldn't give up the ball. I just would not let them take it from me because I was determined to win.

There were times when my coach pulled me out of the pool, out of the game, because he thought the game was getting too physical. I actually love that part of the game.

But that was the way I knew I needed to play. I knew I couldn't out-muscle the other older players, but if I could get a shot off from the perimeter before a defensive player got to me, I knew I was contributing to the team. So letting an opponent steal the ball from me was just not something I was willing to let happen. Water polo is a physical, rough game. If you were going to take the ball from me, you were going to have to more than earn it. We were young and still learning to really play the game, so in efforts to steal the ball, many times it would end up a battle to see if the defender could take the ball. When it came to taking it from me, it wasn't likely. I wasn't doing it with my superior size or strength or style. I wasn't big enough to make the stellar shots. I wasn't big enough to make the stellar saves. But dammit, if I had the ball, you weren't going to get it away from me.

All I had to contribute was my heart, and I gave every bit of that to the game.

Where did that drive come from? Who lit the fire? The raw material was in me, probably from the moment I was born, but it took my first coach, my grandfather, to strike the match and light it.

And then, in all those swimming sessions before my friends were even awake, I learned how to take the fire and use it.

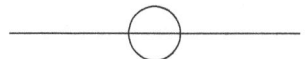

On every team (whether it's a lacrosse team or a corporate committee tasked with solving a certain problem), your best players are your starters. Among those starters, there's always somebody who's the hardest worker—maybe not necessarily your best player, but definitely the hardest worker. Everyone knows who she is. Every day, at practice, or in a game, or in an after-hours work session, this person comes in and gives you her all.

In support of the starters, you have your role players. Behind the role players, you have a few bench warmers who might, with a lot of effort, someday work themselves into the starting lineup. And then you have all the other players, who realize they are destined to spend their entire careers collecting splinters in their butts.

Every team is built this way.

When the role players get settled in their position with no hope of moving up, sometimes they stop working as hard. They will never reach the starting lineup, so why keep trying?

We also see starters who realize that no one's coming up behind them. The role players are not quite good enough to take over the starting spots, so the starters stop worrying about losing their positions, and they ease off on working to get better. And so complacency can settle in on a very good team.

But if the members of the team — if *you* — manage to keep the competitive fire burning, keep your eye on the prize, never stop seeking out inspiration, never forget what it felt like to score your first goal or hit your first three-pointer — then you'll keep digging deep, and you'll keep your career on an upward arc.

As kids, we weren't much inspired by the idea of winning a game. Playing wasn't about winning, as much as it was about running hard, breaking out in a sweat, giggling, chasing after each other, and having a good time.

But eventually, we found ourselves on a team, and all of a sudden, somebody was keeping score. Now there are winners and losers.

Different people respond in different ways to the possibility of losing and the hope of winning.

They bring different personality traits to the table. Some are well suited for competition. Some — not so much.

But those qualities can be nurtured through our childhood sports experiences.

I wasn't aggressive by nature. Far from it. I cried all of the time.

While my cousins and the other kids were doing what I thought were really great things, really fun things, I would sit on the sidelines. My girl cousins seemed so tomboyish to me, running up and down, socking the boys, swinging from tree limbs. And I would just sit off to the side and say, "Are you guys thirsty? Do you want me to fetch you some Kool-Aid?"

The experience of getting beat up on the basketball court forced me to dig deep. It taught me to be find a streak of aggression inside myself that I hadn't known was there.

From my first years in basketball, I was usually the tallest girl on the court. Girls on other teams, taking my size as an invitation to get physical, would shove me and intimidate me.

My first reaction was, I don't like this.

Then, after a while of getting pushed around, I started to ask myself, What do I have to do to stop this? Through a process of trial and error, I found out that if I was aggressive, I could push them back.

I learned to put my elbows out when I pulled down a rebound. I learned to drive them back on their heels. I learned to fill up space so they couldn't shove me.

Then, I realized that my aggressiveness was clearing room around me. They couldn't reach the ball, and I suddenly had space to take a step, or two or three.

So my next question was, What am I going to do with that space?

The obvious answer was, Take the ball to the hoop.

Getting pushed around made me more aggressive, being more aggressive made me a far more effective basketball player, and seeing how I could be more effective — how I was starting to pull down more rebounds and score more points and make more assists—made my competitive drive come to life. It set a fire in me and got my heart going.

Once your heart's beating, I don't believe it's ever really going to stop. The same fire that burned on the basketball court, the soccer field, or the running track is still in there. After years of not being tended, it may be smoldering, kind of low and dim, but I believe it's still there, way down deep, waiting for you to apply it to a new challenge.

I encourage everyone to remember the way the adrenaline flowed when they competed in sports. That same competitive drive is still there, ready to impel you forward on the trajectory of your career.

Some of us are born with a relentless work ethic. We're bred-in-the-bone Type A personalities. We don't need to go looking for inspiration. It has a way of finding us.

But there is an important aspect of the work ethic that is learned, too, just like you learned to make contact with a baseball or sink a free throw.

As a kid, I used to get up early for swim practice, then go to school, and then go to swim practice again after school.

Meanwhile, my friends were rolling out of bed just in time to make the first bell.

My life was really different.

It wasn't always fun. There were lots of mornings when I really wanted to roll over and fall back asleep. But that wasn't how my life was structured. That work ethic became part of who I am.

My coach constantly challenged me to do much more than I thought I could. Some people rise to that challenge, and some people don't.

I arrived before the rest of the team, and Coach would challenge me to swim a certain number of laps. I would think, *Oh, my God! I'm going to die.* I mean, he set such a high bar for me. But I tell you what: when I swam in a meet, I would hit the wall, and before I turned to watch my competitors still finishing, I would look up at Mike. That's when I knew that the work was worth it.

That work ethic stuck with me when I was a single parent, working my way up and competing with people who didn't have the same kinds of responsibilities at home. It was more of a sacrifice for me to go in as early and stay as late as my colleagues, but it felt natural to me to make that sacrifice. After all, I'd been making that kind of sacrifice for years and years, beginning with my childhood swimming days.

Later on, when I went back and studied for my MBA ... well, that was a huge challenge to keep all the balls in the air, a tremendous sacrifice, but it felt natural, and of course it was worth it. My relentless work ethic told me, *This is not too much, you can do this, it's worth it.*

Lately, I've been working on my Ph.D. with the same kind of schedule.

The same sort of sacrifice.

The person who's faced with this kind of challenge for the first time in her mid-twenties is going to be, in a word, lost.

But if you've been through it before—if you learned this sort of relentless work ethic as a young athlete—it's natural to look upon the sacrifices as little more than an inconvenience.

It will feel natural to you to focus on the end result, rather than on the pain and sacrifice.

You're going to dive in head first, because that's what you've always done.

It felt very much the same walking into a room at a company that ran at a loss for the last five years, looking around at my new people, and saying, "This is the amount of revenue that we're going to generate from sales this year."

People looked at me like I must be smoking something. That would take about two seconds, then there was this realization: "Oh, my God! She's serious."

Just like Mike knew I was capable of meeting his challenge, I knew those companies and those people were capable of what I was challenging them to do. Now it was time to get to work, and I could tell from the expression on people's faces which ones were up to the challenge and which were not.

I believe that a relentless work ethic is a form of muscle memory. Once you've practiced it for a certain number of hours, it becomes natural.

Ever since my swimming days, that's how I play a game. It's also how I run a business.

That's why you played with everything you had to give.

That's why you stay up late, honing your big presentation to perfection. That's why you refuse to take the path of least resistance.

That's why some people do the things that differentiate them from the crowd.

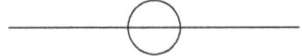

Remember what it was like to be an athlete, at the end of a hard workout. Your toes might have been blistered, your arches hurt, your muscles screamed, your lungs ached — but it felt so damn good!

Remember what it was like, and re-ignite the relentless work ethic that made you a winner on the playing field.

In your work life, let it drive you to stay in the game, show up, and work with tenacity and intensity and drive and heart.

There's no point in trying to exert leadership on the basketball court or the soccer field before you've achieved mastery of the basic skills of the game. Likewise, what top manager is going to give you a chance to lead if you don't have a clue about finance, technology management, and marketing?

Even during the busiest years of my basketball career, I knew I wanted to be successful, post-basketball, in business. But I had learned, on the basketball court, that you don't acquire an essential skill-set just by wishing. You have to decide to become competent. You have to practice, study, work at it. You have to work so, so hard.

Even while I was playing, I worked on my M.B.A. During the off-season, I would do my gym routine, attend classes, do homework late into the night, and get up the next morning to do it all over again.

People would tell me, "You're doing too much. You're going to burn out. You're not having any fun."

But my response was always, "It's a sacrifice now, but I'm totally willing to make it, because I know I am going to need these competencies to reach my goals in the next stage of my career."

If you feel like the end-game—the state championship, the successful transformation of your corporate division, your climb from the mailroom to the boardroom—is just too far away, you may need to break it down into manageable pieces.

Give yourself a goal for the next game, or the next week, or the next fiscal year. Focus on achieving that manageable goal. Use it to inspire yourself. Use it to light a fire inside yourself.

When you have that kind of fire crackling inside you, there's no obstacle that's going to stop you.

It may slow you down, maybe, but it will never, never stop you.

When I first became a professional basketball player, I had been in New York working on my modeling career, and basketball was the furthest thing from my mind. I didn't take the WNBA very seriously. I thought it was going to be something like a summer league, and I believed my size, my skills, and all my years of playing would be more than enough to see me through. I figured I could just show up and play.

So I came in totally unprepared, stepped into a league full of really talented women who were taking it a lot more seriously than I was, and that first year I played nowhere near my standards. It was embarrassing, and I was miserable all season long. I decided if I'm going to play in the WNBA, I'm going to do it right.

The WNBA season was during the summer, so I was going to have to figure out a way to prepare the rest of the year. I hired a trainer, who got me on a proper meal plan and taught me how to fuel my body. I would get up at 6:00 so I could meet my trainer at 6:34 a.m. for an hour and a half of lifting weights and cross training. I'd come home and rest, then head back to the gym and play pickup basketball with Magic Johnson and a bunch of other pro players.

It was challenging, but I knew I had to put into my sport what I wanted to get out of it. I've never been sorry for completely dedicating myself to my craft, even though I sacrificed so many fun times for it. I wasn't balanced socially. I didn't get to hang out all the time. I missed out on so many occasions, from graduations to parties. I made the sacrifice to head to the gym instead. I've known a lot of men and women early in their business careers who would claim they were totally serious about the trajectory of their careers, but they wanted their fun, they wanted their me-time.

Sorry, guys: if you really, truly want to be successful, you have to be relentless, in your effort and your desire, at whatever it is you're trying to do.

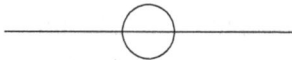

Right now, at this very minute, one of your opponents is in a gym in Brazil refining her jump shot.

Right now, an executive from your main competitor is polishing up a plan to steal away your biggest customer.

What are you going to do about it?

Go home early, or keep yourself in the game?

In the state championship final, I missed the game-winning shot.

I remember that failure so well, as if it were yesterday. I moped around with tears in my eyes, until my mom told me, "It's up to you. You can lie on your bed and cry, or you can get up and do something about it."

That's what it took — my mom telling me to get back in the game.

So I headed back to the gym, shot 500 baskets a day, and played pickup with anybody who would play with me, two on two, three on three, five on five, men, women, kids. It didn't matter.

That was how I responded to losing when I was a young girl, and that lesson stuck with me in my pro career. We lost to the Comets in the Western Conference playoffs four years in a row, but it was always a learning opportunity. It made me think: What could I have done better? How can I play better? How can I help my teammates get better?

Most times, you fail before you win. A lot of times, people don't notice you until you're at the top, and they don't realize all the failed attempts that came before.

The same thing happens in business. There have been thousands of start-up companies that have failed, but those companies' founding entrepreneurs have learned from their failures and gone on to incredible successes.

Failure doesn't have to be the end. In fact, it's an essential step on the path to success.

You need to look back, re-evaluate, practice, work harder, plan harder, and get better.

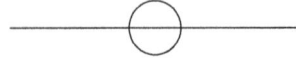

We don't always do a great job of raising the bar for ourselves.

We don't always motivate and challenge ourselves to work hard and become better.

What we need, sometimes, is to go out and find somebody who's going to push us hard and help us get better.

I was a soccer goal-keeper, and among my teammates were some talented women with the speed and strength to take really great shots at me. I would work my tail off in practice, but eventually I got the sense that I was limiting myself.

So, I started staying after practice and taking shots with the guys' team. The guys' keeper and I would swap off, five shots in the net, then switching off, rotating back and forth.

The girls were just as accurate as the guys, so I was used to tracking the attacker, breaking fast to one side or the other, leaping for the corners, knocking the ball away. None of that was new to me.

But those guys kicked so much harder than the girls. I have to tell you, as a keeper on women's teams, you don't know how to save a goal until you defend against a guy. He kicks that ball so damn hard.

Often, the biggest lesson didn't come from making the save. It was learning not to grimace, learning to hide how much it hurt when I made the save because the ball was coming at me so hard.

By challenging myself, I made myself better. Think of it as running in ankle weights. When you take them off, you've gained strength and speed.

When I got back on the soccer field with the women, things felt like they were happening a little bit slower. The game was just a little bit more manageable. My coach knew it, my teammates knew it, and pretty soon, my opponents got to know it, too.

All right, you may be saying. Good soccer story. Next time I'm keeper for a women's soccer team, I'll keep it in mind.

But what does challenging yourself — raising the bar—in soccer have to do with success in business?

I'm reminded of my early days at ASUG, the largest trade association on the globe supporting SAP clients. SAP boasts tens of billions of euros a year in revenues. The client base is impressively large.

I have been on the scene to clean up some nasty corporate messes, so believe me when I tell you, this was a classic failure in process. Liquidity was a huge issue that I had to get my arms around before any turnaround effort could begin. The organization was facing collapse, everything was "on fire," and because the board had waited too long to bring in a turnaround specialist (me), we were literally out of time. Every little screw-up, no matter how trivial, might be the one that broke the camel's back.

To get a better view of how we were interacting with the hundreds of thousands of SAP customers we represented, I decided to attend one of our specialty events. The event had about 5,000 people in attendance. They had paid an average of $2,500 for the weekend.

As soon as I arrived, I noticed a staff member dealing with a frustrated attendee. After their exchange, I asked the staff member to tell me about the issue. In a tone I would later coach my team never to use when addressing customer frustration, she explained, "Apparently, the attendee didn't get the vegetarian meal she ordered."

Big deal, right?

Well, yes. To that individual, it was a big deal. A really big deal.

We had a speaker who represented Coca-Cola, and I was surprised—horrified—to realize that the only refreshments in the back of his lecture room were Pepsi products. To that speaker, it was going to be a gigantic big deal.

I had staff who'd been with the organization for a long time, and they'd been trained to work at about 50% of full speed. Maybe 70% on a good day. No wonder the company was failing.

I have to say, I don't think this was representative of their abilities. Rather, it was a result of leadership. For the most part, they were talented, dedicated people. They were simply responding to expectations. No one had ever told them, "Give it your all." What they'd been hearing was, 'Pretty good is good enough."

Well, I gathered them together and said, "We're going to work as hard as we have to, and we're going to do this job as close to perfect as it's possible to do. I want you to work as if this matters — because it does."

They sort of shrugged their shoulders, as if they were too busy to deal with things like that.

Like I said, not their fault. It's just what they were used to.

"What about the Pepsi products in the Coke speaker's room?" I asked.

A group shrug.

I pointed to several of my staff members. "I saw a grocery store around the corner," I said.

"So?"

"Buy the whole store out of Coca-Cola."

"Now?"

"Yes. Right now."

The shrugs turned into grins, and those staff members were off in a flash.

Then I told my staff to up their game — to work harder — to fix every problem ... and to fix it now!

I empowered them to fix every problem the minute it came up, and they were to document every problem they fixed so I could send an apology letter to that attendee's room before 10 that evening. The rule became, "No one goes to bed while problems exist."

My staff members looked around at each other, and from the looks in their eyes, I could tell: This person has the heart for this way of doing things. She's getting her game face on. But this other person? Not so much.

It was a lot like athletics, when the competition will not give you time to regroup. If you're getting thumped, you don't get to go home, get a good night's sleep, and figure out how you're going to be better the next day. You have to stay in the game, work as hard as you have to, and make it work.

Some of my people had trouble adapting to the new way of doing things.

They lacked the heart. They didn't last long. I wish them well.

But others shifted gears almost instantly. They accepted my challenge. It was as if they had really been wanting to work their hardest. They had just been waiting all this time for permission to show their stuff.

I have no way of confirming my suspicion, but I'm willing to bet that those who succeeded in the new ASUG had sports backgrounds.

They were like high jumpers when the bar gets raised to a new height. Some of them look up in horror and think, *I've never jumped that high.* Others look up and think, *I can!*

Attacking a challenge with heart and a relentless work ethic was totally familiar to them.

We worked harder, we became a team, and customer satisfaction went up 20 points over the course of 24 months, our revenue grew substantially, and our profitability was restored.

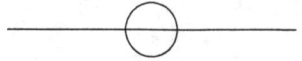

Chalk Talk
- Chapter 2 -

* DIG DOWN DEEP

* RELENTLESS
WORK ETHIC

* RAISE THE BAR
(SELF-MOTIVATE)

CHAPTER THREE

———

Have a Winning Attitude

(F-it: the Three Fs)

When playing sports, you learned that you were going nowhere without a winning attitude.

It's the same in the office. Without a winning attitude, you're going nowhere.

In our athletic lives and in our business lives, we've identified three consistent attributes of a winning attitude. We call them the Three Fs (and, with a knowing smile, we punctuate each one with an enthusiastic: *F-it!*).

They are: Be **Firm**.

Be **Friendly**. Be **Fair**.

We've found that when we manage to demonstrate each of those qualities, we possess a winning attitude that our teammates and our competitors notice right away.

We always try to approach every situation with passion and intensity—and we try to shrug off the negatives, too (because there *will* be negatives).

That's how we maintain our game faces.

We urge you to use Firm, Friendly, and Fair to create a winning game face, too.

What do we mean by "game face?"

Think of it as an attitude that's expressed in your face, your body language, your choice of words, your tone of voice, and your overall approach. Your game face says, *I'm not here just to wear the uniform or collect the paycheck.* It doesn't say you're arrogant, but it does say, *I'm here to perform!*

In 2002, the team that stood between us and the WNBA Finals was Sacramento. Coop told us this semifinal game was going to be the toughest challenge we faced all year, and within a few minutes, we knew we were in for a real dog fight.

I started out playing the game that had got us there: fade-away jumpers and jump shots.

But Coop called a time out, and when we gathered around him, he gave me a super-serious look and said, "Not today, Smooth."

Huh? Don't play my game?

"That shit isn't going to do it today."

That shit?

"Get in there and take the hits," he said. "Use your power moves on the block. Let them know you're bringing it. It's winning time."

Oh, so that's what he meant!

He wanted me to play fair, like always, but also to show up firm with the game face that said, to our opponents, my teammates, our fans, and even to myself, "Today, I'm going to do exactly what I need to do to win this game."

And win we did!

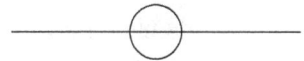

It wasn't about being arrogant. It was about saying, *Hey, everybody. If I were you, I'd start planning on seeing the very best of me!*

When you adjust your game face — when you pull on the costume of a warrior — you're delivering a message to your opponents. *Be afraid. Be very afraid.*

You're delivering a message to your teammates or colleagues, too.

Count on me.

And don't forget one more important person: yourself. Without saying a word to yourself (or sometimes with a few well-chosen, well- timed expletives under your breath), you ratchet up your own confidence. You feel the power welling up from somewhere deep inside. Your level of aggression rises a few degrees. You're ready for the game, the project, the meeting — anything the world has to throw at you.

After you've been in the game for a while, you'll probably discover that you possess half a dozen different game faces.

That's great, because sometimes you're going to need an absolutely thoughtful demeanor, sometimes your voice and expression need to express empathy, and sometimes a growl is going to be most effective. The challenge is to remember which game face is appropriate for any given situation.

Remember this situation (or one an awful lot like it)? An opponent has been throwing elbows, disrupting your shooting, and throwing you off your game. Your coach brings you out for a quick breather, and while you're sitting on the bench, you consider how you're going to go back into the game. Will you storm in with your hands clenched into fists and glare at your opponent with anger written all over your face? Or will you straighten yourself up a little bit, keep your eyes averted from your opponent, turn to your teammates, and say, with confidence, *"Let's get this done!"*?

There may be times when game face #1 will shake your opponent's confidence. Other times, game face #2 is what you need to help your team ratchet up their game.

In a strategy session, a colleague may head off in a direction that you absolutely know is the wrong way to go. Do you respond with a brutal game face and snarl, "You don't know what you're talking about, do you?" — or do you settle into a game face that's a combination of empathy, thoughtfulness, and firmness?

There are lots of different effective game faces, but all of them have several things in common. First, a game face is like getting into a suit of armor. It involves protecting yourself from, removing, shrugging off, or ignoring the distractions that disrupt cool, calm planning and successful implementation.

The firm, effective game face has a way of communicating, "You can throw anything you want at me, but I'm not going to take it personally." Keep in mind: it isn't about you. What's important is the game or the match; it's about getting the job done.

Opponents will react to every flaw in your game. When you're having an off game, fans will express their displeasure. In the workplace, people will talk. It's human nature.

And don't imagine for a second that workplace politics or dynamics won't turn your colleagues (the people who are supposed to be your loyal collaborators) into competitors — sometimes, sneaky ones. You need the right approach.

When you make people unhappy, they will piss and moan about you. And remember, some people will be unhappy with you, no matter what you do or what you expect of them. But keep this in mind: Watercooler talk is not actionable feedback. It's just distracting noise.

It's human nature to defend yourself, too. After all, you have feelings.

No one enjoys being criticized.

But one aspect of wearing your game face is to deal with criticism in the firmest, most effective manner. Nearly always, in our experience, the wisest, most effective way of dealing with criticism is to adjust your game face, decide that your armor is made of Teflon, ignore the "watercooler talk," shrug off the "bad press," hide that your feelings sometimes can get hurt (because you're human, too), remind yourself that "bad publicity is better than no publicity," and let the complaining, criticizing, and Monday morning quarterbacking run its course. When you ignore the noise, it just won't be as much fun to criticize you anymore. People will soon get bored, they'll decide there's no story there, and the chattering will fade to silence.

This is true for a high school athlete or a corporate CEO … and just as true for an A-list entertainer.

On a cold day with the temperature dropping rapidly, and with no opportunity to rehearse with the U.S. Marine Corps Band, Beyoncé decided to do what she had to do to make one of the most important, most visible, and definitely most challenging performances of her life come off perfectly. At Barack Obama's January 2013 inauguration, she sang The Star-Spangled Banner, a challenging song under the best of conditions, to a crowd of hundreds of thousands gathered on the National Mall and many millions more watching on television. Millions were stunned by the perfection and energy of her rendition. For nearly everyone who heard her, it was a highlight of a remarkable day.

People rarely leave a good thing alone. Shortly after the event, it was leaked that Beyoncé's performance was not 100% live. She had sung along with a recording of herself singing the anthem. This led to speculation that she might not have been singing at all. She might have been lip-syncing the entire performance.

There was an enormous uproar, all across the blogosphere and the Twitter universe. The implication was that she had done something horribly wrong and deceitful. Commentators were quick to call this a Milli Vanilli moment (remember them?), even though the two situations had almost nothing in common.

Of course, Beyoncé would use these same skills we are discussing in this chapter to illustrate what a top-shelf, top-class professional should do in such an unfortunate scenario. Beyoncé didn't get defensive. She didn't lie. She didn't make excuses. She put on her own Teflon game face and answered her critics in the best way possible — by performing. During an unforgettable press conference, Beyoncé calmly provided perspective with class and dignity. She also treated a room full of reporters to an incredible a cappella version of the National Anthem. After she finished the last note, it was clear the matter was closed.

Then she followed it up with a remarkable version of the National Anthem at the Super Bowl.

The "scandal" surrounding the inauguration National Anthem? A forgotten blip in an amazing career.

Yet another thing about an effective game face is that it's about being smarter, not louder. It means keeping your emotions in check. Stay calm. Don't get upset. Refuse to get angry. It means, as one of our grandfathers taught us, playing chess, rather than checkers. Keep your emotions in check so you can think several moves ahead.

The rise of female professionals through the business ranks is something many of us take for granted these days. Sure, we still face challenges that are specific to women. We're under no illusions about that, but we begin our careers optimistic that we'll be rewarded for hard work and talent.

And then we discover, to our disappointment, that it's still not an even playing field.

Not even close.

What we learn is that the corporate world is still a largely masculine environment. The successful men we observe usually possess "typical male qualities:" aggression, arrogance, emotional coldness, pure analytical focus, lack of empathy, and putting ends ahead of means. Men who behave this way are widely admired. "He's a real man's man," people say. "He's a strong executive."

We use these men as our role models, or we find female role models who, in their own early careers, used "men's men" as *their* role models. These women became aggressive, arrogant, emotionally cold, and all the rest. They became "hyper-masculine." They became — excuse the language, but it's what they're nearly always called — *bitches.*

Now, if you're an early-career businesswoman, it's your turn. As you search for role models of success, you may find yourself doing the same thing, modeling yourself after a man's man or a bitch.

We suggest a different, better way.

Women — *as women* — have far too much to offer. Too much is lost when a talented woman sets aside all the qualities that make up her femininity.

Though some old-school businessmen (and even businesswomen) still don't believe it, introducing a woman into the boardroom, into an executive position, or into any leadership role, tends to change things—dramatically, and almost always for the better. The frat-boy mentality fades away. We put people at ease. We stoke creativity in the room. Communication improves. Attention to customer needs increases. Employee satisfaction improves.

This is not to say that every "typically female quality" is universally always productive. We've used the word "bitch." Now, give us a just little more linguistic freedom: Some women tend to *nag.*

Ouch — but it's true. Instead of coming right out and saying, "This is the right way to do this, and this is what we're going to do," some of us have a tendency to natter on and on about why it needs to be this way. We so badly want everyone to come along with us of their own free will. We want everyone to like us. We want consensus. We want everyone to understand the *why* of a decision, but it may be that our people only need to know the *what*: "This is *what* we're going to do."

When a woman lays down the law to her colleagues or her subordinates, what response should she expect? Her people will file out of the meeting room, and before they've walked half a dozen steps down the corridor, someone (a man, probably, but sometimes a woman, too) will mutter, "The bitch."

If you overhear that *sotto voce* snarl, your feelings are going to be hurt, aren't they? We're all human, after all. We all want to be liked.

But being called a "bitch" occasionally, like it or not, is a signal that we are being effective in our leadership. It is a sign of firmness.

Just keep in mind that there's a difference between "being bitchy" and "being a bitch." Being bitchy is rarely productive, but being a bitch is *not* a bad thing. It may leave a wake behind her, but it gets things done.

Here is what we advise early-career women: Lead off with your feminine side. Wear the game face of a smart, talented, goal-oriented, but *definitely feminine* woman. When you walk into the meeting room or boardroom, seek to facilitate open communication. Be happy if you are able to help achieve consensus (because consensus is a good thing— until it's not).

But keep another game face in reserve. Keep it in your pocket, ready to it pull out and put it on. We're talking about the game face of the bitch.

Take advantage of being a woman, but when it's time to lay down the law, time to say "This is the *what* of the situation, the *why* doesn't concern you, and the buck stops with me," then be prepared to hear "Bitch" muttered as your people walk away.

If you've donned your Teflon-bitch game face, you'll be fine. Better than fine. You'll be great!

One of the important things we learned in athletics was to be **fair** to our teammates.

Being fair meant trusting them to perform.

No player, no matter how talented and well trained, can single-handedly perform every necessary skill on the basketball court or the soccer field, so we had to trust our teammate to catch the ball. Even if she missed the first one, we needed to try again. We needed to be fair with her, in order to build that essential trust and camaraderie.

Likewise, no matter what sort of business genius you may be, you'll never be the expert in all of the dozen functional areas that every successful project requires. Being fair to your colleagues means trusting them enough to delegate, treating them with respect, and demonstrating to them that they can trust you to be there for them.

Sometimes we find ourselves doubting that our people will give it the same 100% effort that we will. As a result, we find ourselves taking on the marketing, and taking on the finances, and taking on the logistics, and so on and so on.

"If you want something done right, you have to do it yourself." Right?

No.

If you want everything that needs doing to be done, then you need to be fair enough to trust in your teammates.

When you move from athletics to the corporate environment, the lesson is the same, though you'll discover that risk tolerance in a corporate leadership role can be very different from risk tolerance on the baseball field, the ice hockey rink, or the tennis court. Being fair in business has nuances that are not quite the same as in athletics. You may need to re-learn trust.

I had a really wonderful young executive, one of those remarkable guys who thought through every process from top to bottom, smartly calculated the risks and rewards, and then forged ahead under the principle that it was better to ask forgiveness than to ask for permission. This is an attitude that simply can't be taught.

At the beginning of the year or the beginning of the quarter, I would throw a challenge at him and say, "I really don't want to talk about how you're going to get this done, unless you need to come to me and work through something, but I've got your back if it comes to that."

One time, he put in place a project that ruffled a lot of feathers, and I got an angry phone call from the chair and the vice chair. I told them, "I made that decision, and I asked him to launch that project. My thoughts were this. My learning was that. He was working on my behalf, and I trust him totally. Thanks for your feedback. We're making some adjustments."

He was sitting right across my desk during that phone call, and he heard every word I said.

Our level of trust, which had already been high, expanded enormously.

Chalk Talk
- Chapter 3 -

* FIRM

* FRIENDLY

* FAIR

CHAPTER FOUR

Share the Glory

I f you never lose sight of the fact that everyone on the team has something to contribute, then you won't risk wasting valuable resources. If you practice humility, you won't risk turning someone from a potentially valuable teammate (if not today or tomorrow, then maybe someday) into an adversary. And if you keep from getting too big for your britches ... well, you won't risk splitting your seams when you bend over.

Leadership, even if you've absorbed it through years of competition, isn't easy.

It's always worth the effort, but never easy.

The leader finds herself in front of the room with everyone's eyes on her. She is everyone's target.

Succeed, and you'll be expected to share the glory. Fail, and it will land squarely on your shoulders.

That's a difficult situation for anyone, but far, far more difficult for someone who has never experienced anything like it.

Fortunately, we've been there. In athletics, we learned how to share the glory with our teammates. We learned to hunker down and work twice as hard to rebound from failure. And, we learned that everyone on the team has contributions to make. Don't hog the ball, whether you're on the basketball court or in the corporate world. Every team performs better when everyone is empowered to contribute and when everyone shares collectively in the win. Neither of us has ever been sorry for sharing the glory.

I remember a game in middle school, when we were taking it to our arch-rival team. Not only were we beating them, but it was one of those games when I was playing out of my head. I could do no wrong, scoring every time I got my hands on the ball. Pretty good for a point guard. I was awesome.

And then, out of the blue, for no reason at all, our coach yanked me out of the game.

"I don't remember this being the Bridgette Team," she told me.

Huh? I was being a one-girl wrecking crew. Wasn't the point to get the ball in the hoop as many times as we could? I didn't get it.

"Seriously? You're taking me out? Are you kidding me?"

But she wasn't kidding. She made me ride the bench for the rest of the game.

I was so pissed, I don't even remember whether we finally won or lost the game. But I sure do remember getting yanked. The coach's name was Lori Junewick. I even remember what she was wearing that day.

Coach Junewick taught me a lesson I've never forgotten. She essentially told me, "This is a team sport, not a stage for one player to show off. I'd rather lose as a team than have one player hog all the glory."

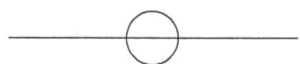

Kids are natural ball hogs.

They all picture themselves as the star of the team, the one who's single-handedly dribbling down the court and tossing up the game-winning shot.

It's just in the nature of young players.

It's the coach's job to stifle that childish impulse and instill teamwork in her players. It's a difficult lesson to learn, even harder to teach, but a great coach knows how to teach her kids that it's more satisfying to win as a team than to score a lot of points and walk off the court in defeat. We got to experience it in our own early athletic days, and more recently, we've watched our daughters' coaches showing them that when the players work together, make two, three, or four passes, and get everyone in position … the game flows along so much smoother.

It's one of the best feelings in the world to walk off the court at the end of the game as a team of winners.

It's the same in business, isn't it? It's such a great feeling to share success with your colleagues.

We Need to Talk, on CBS Sports Network, is a first in the world of sports journalism: an all-women sports show.

But it's not just a slightly nuanced take on a typical sports gab-fest. We Need to Talk features not three or four, but twelve women on-camera. And these aren't just any female sports fans. These are high-powered women from all sorts of athletic backgrounds: correspondents and analysts and sports anchors, Olympic swimmers and basketball players, a professional tennis player, a boxing champion, and executives with professional leagues. Not only that, but all of the show's producers and directors are women, too.

The potential for an incredible show was there.

But so was the potential for a monumental, very public flop.

I came to the process with a closet full of sports awards, but in that room, I was just one out of a dozen highly accomplished women.

Every one of us had spent plenty of time in the spotlight. Every one of us enjoyed it. That's the kind of accomplished women we were.

It could easily have disintegrated into a melee of clashing egos — but it didn't.

I walked into that room, deliberately, from a humble place. As we worked toward the show's premiere date, I realized that these other women, each with their own closet full of sports awards, had each made the same decision: to come from a humble place.

The process simply would not have worked, otherwise.

We prepared with the sort of single-minded intensity that you'd expect from such a team. We worked together, supporting each other, contributing in every way we could.

And then, the evening arrived.

Every one of us was accustomed to the spotlight, but there was a nervous tension in the air.

I wondered, *What can I contribute? How can I lead?*

"Hey, hey, listen up everybody," I said. Then when every eye was on me, I said, "We're all here together, and we are only going to be as successful as the next person sitting next to us. Every one of us knows all about teamwork, don't we? So let's work together, do our best, and have some fun!"

All my colleagues started cheering, and from that moment, we were a team!

The lights went on. The cameras rolled. We talked games, scores, personalities, and issues that mattered to us as athletes, sports fans, and women. These things apparently matter to a large audience, too. We Need to Talk has been called "attention grabbing," "insightful," and "groundbreaking," and it's been picked up for another year.

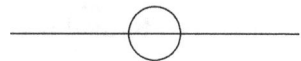

Admittedly, not every member of your team is going to be 100% deserving. Sometimes, you will find yourself working with a difficult teammate, someone lacking the drive, the will, or the team spirit to perform to her highest. You're going to find yourself in a situation where a colleague brings with him a cloud of pointless bad energy: "This won't work; we're doomed to failure. What's the point of trying?" It's simply inevitable — it's part of playing with others.

In surveys of Fortune 500 companies, more than 50% admit to having this kind of "cultural cancer." She may seem to be wearing your team jersey, but she's definitely not a member of your team. She drags everyone down and impedes success. She may withhold resources or even try to sabotage your project. But — for various reasons, perhaps because she's the company's primary client's best friend — everyone is afraid to "vote her off the island."

There are several schools of thoughts about how to handle such a (very common) situation.

Some leaders, only able to see the immediate short-term implication, allow the cancerous individual to remain in place, ambushing people in meetings, kicking important subordinates out of projects, hogging all the credit, and taking all the commissions.

Other leaders say, "You know what? The cost of keeping this individual is too great. For the health of the organization, we need to cut our ties to this individual. Working together, we can replace the revenue (or replace her points on the basketball court)."

But there's yet another way to deal with such a situation.

When I've had to deal with a difficult teammate, colleague, or employee, I've always taken the approach of engaging them even more.

My thinking has always been to try to figure out how I could strengthen an interpersonal relationship with her, building trust and hopefully bringing her back around.

If I had a teammate who wasn't shooting well, for example, I would approach her privately and ask, "What are your goals? What do you want to achieve here?"

When you ask someone that question, you may hear aspirations about the job.

On the other hand, you may learn that they couldn't care less.

When I learned an underperforming teammate's basketball goal, I would tell her, "Hey, I'm here to help you achieve that goal. Just meet me in the morning, or let's stay after practice."

Once I had that player's commitment, I would try to figure out what she needed to live up to her potential. Was she better shooting from a dribble or was she a stand-and-shoot type? Where did she like to pass? Especially, why was she giving less than 100%?

The same thing applies in business, doesn't it? You don't put a person who hates numbers in charge of finances; if she's a people-person, you might put her in a position where she's dealing with customers. By delving into the person's hopes and aspirations, you discover where she belongs, what will motivate her, and how to gain her trust.

In basketball, by figuring out the strengths and weaknesses of each of my teammates, I built relationships of trust with everyone.

The result? Team chemistry. We became a successful team.

It worked in basketball, and I've had a lot of success applying the very same strategy to my business career.

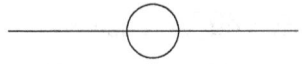

Now, take a moment to call to mind the very best team you were ever on. We're not talking about your best individual athletic achievement; what we have in mind is the very best *team* you ever played on. It might have been a Division 1 championship team, an NAIA small-college team, a semi-pro ball club, or even a middle-school flag-football team.

We're willing to bet that there were supremely talented individuals on that team, and moderately talented role players, and somewhat less talented bench warmers. We're also willing to bet that the members of that team supported each other, encouraged each other, celebrated each other's accomplishments, and treated each other with genuine respect. We'll make that wager with confidence, because that's the character of every great team we've ever been associated with.

The social environment of that very best team of yours made it possible for every teammate to fulfill her talents, play to her potential, be the complete, full, wonderful person she was meant to be, and work together as a finely tuned team.

That team, we'll bet, was characterized by humility.

Let's consider the word "humility" for a moment. Often, people think humility means having an "Oh, I'm not so good" attitude.

That's not at all what we mean by it.

Our notion of humility is one that starts off with, "I'm pretty darn good, aren't I?" But then it continues: "So are you — and if we work together, we can be a team (or a corporation, or a business division, or an office) that is greater than the sum of its parts. We can be incredible!" We are thinking of a form of humility in which you exercise your leadership abilities without imposing on others. We're thinking of a place in which everyone appreciates what everyone else has to share. It's a place where everyone, no matter what their formal role, is empowered to contribute to the group's common goals.

It's a place where you value and respect everyone.

It's a place where you frequently hear, "Good job!" and "Thank you!"

We believe you should do these things and behave this way because they make the team function smoothly, because they are the right thing to do, and, most of all, because they reflect the quality of your character. There's another thing we like to keep in mind: the lady in the mailroom has the potential to become your boss someday, and there may come a time when you'll wish you'd treated her with respect.

> When I played for the Los Angeles Sparks, some players couldn't be bothered to carry their sweaty uniforms to the basket. Instead, they would simply drop their gear on the floor. The team manager, who was responsible for washing our things, would have to put on gloves, pick up the uniforms from the floor, and carry them to the laundry.
>
> I always made a point of carrying my things to the basket. A small thing, right?
>
> After all, cleaning up after the players was part of the team manager's job.
>
> There really was no upside to carrying my stuff to the basket—except for one minor detail.
>
> Coach Thompson, who started as the Sparks' team manager in 1997, rose to become head coach of the Sparks and then head coach of the Houston Comets.
>
> Some of those players who were too lazy — and not humble enough — to put their dirty gear in the basket later wished they had.
>
> I've never, ever been unhappy about treating another person with respect, dignity, and integrity.

Being the best, posting the huge statistics, and running the fastest time, automatically gives an athlete a certain amount of "mojo," but it doesn't make her a leader. There are plenty of incredibly skilled athletes who lack a dribble of team spirit. They work just hard enough to be the best on the field (even though they have the talent to be something really special). They are in it for their own glory. In their opinion, their teammates are only there to be bit players in their own personal drama.

In our experience, this type typically enjoys a couple of years as the "big man (or woman) on campus." Sadly, her life trajectory often peaks in her late teenage years, and she never manages to fulfill the promise of her early years. She might have been a star athlete, but she never learned the lessons that were there for the taking. She never got any joy out of winning as a team; she never realized that a team can make it a lot farther than an individual, no matter how talented; she never figured out that starring is not the same as leading; she thought of lazy shortcuts as effective strategies; she never experienced failure, because she didn't really share in her team's wins and losses; she never understood how to make the players around her better.

In the business world, you will encounter individuals who feel the need to speak in the first person, rather than as part of the collective. They simply never learned to say, "This is what my colleague came up with," or "This is what our team achieved." Instead, it's always, "I, I, I ..." After all, the credit is there for the grabbing, isn't it?

They seem to believe that by taking all the credit, they are going to get ahead faster than the poor slobs who are too "timid" to grab all the credit.

To which we say, "Bull."

This might have been true once upon a time (*Mad Men*, anyone?), but today's successful businesses tend to operate with a spirit of teamwork in which it's vital to share credit.

If you are a member of a work team, it's important to understand and appreciate not just your own role, but everyone else's role, too. If you are the leader, it's important to make sure everyone feels like they are the critical cog in the wheel that makes the entire mechanism turn smoothly.

This isn't to say that all organizations are the same or that all individuals have the same personality traits and working styles. Some people work well in a traditional hierarchy, some thrive in a flatter organization, and some are finding their place in an experimental environment, such as the "holacracy" at Zappo's. A holacracy is characterized by an absence of job titles and an emphasis on information, ideas, and innovation flowing not only up and down, but in all directions at once.

Whatever the athletic team or corporate environment, we are convinced that it is most productive in the long run to respect everyone, to empower everyone, and always to thank people for their contributions (especially when they are not expecting to be singled out).

Did you have a chance to see Kevin Durant's MVP acceptance speech in 2014? If not, we encourage you to check it out at www. youtube.com / watch?v=jrL-LYJ9afQ.

This was a shining moment for Durant. Everyone had come to see him, listen to him, congratulate him, tell him how awesome he was, and bask in a little bit of his glory.

Did he talk about how hard he'd worked, how he'd overcome long odds, how special he was?

No, he didn't.

Durant took advantage of his moment in the spotlight to talk about his brother, his friends, and especially his mother.

His mom?

He thanked her for her sacrifices. He remembered the times when she had gone hungry so he could eat. He said, "I wouldn't be here without you."

In his speech, Durant summed up what we're talking about here. Even when you know how much you've contributed to a project or a business success, when you get the microphone, it's time to say, "*We* completed this, and it wouldn't have happened without ..." And then you name your people and itemize their contributions: the ideas, the late nights, the enthusiasm, the ... *whatever.*

When I had my quarterly executive leadership meetings, I would expect every vice president to bring to the meeting an example of somebody who was struggling and what they were doing to improve that person's performance; and, I expected every v.p. to bring an example of one of their reports who was hitting it out of the ballpark.

Right there in the executive meeting, I would make a phone call to that superstar. I would say, "Hey, listen, I'm sitting here with the vice president of your division. He's telling me about this incredible initiative, how you really took it to the finish line, and I've just got to tell you I'm crazy impressed and want to thank you for your hard work."

These individuals would be so astonished.

Chalk Talk
- Chapter 4 -

* EVERYONE CAN CONTRIBUTE

* PRACTICE HUMILITY

* DON'T GET TOO BIG FOR YOUR BRITCHES (as my Grandpa would say)

CHAPTER FIVE

Perseverance

In tough times, who are you?

Shrug off the emotion, because it isn't personal. Set incremental goals and achieve them one by one. Learn from your failures — after all, you've already paid for them.

We like to say: *Perfection is about your intention. Failure is about your character.*

It's our experience that you don't learn much about people when you're winning. Moving from success to success is the easy part.

But who are you when you're losing? Do you throw in the towel, or do you persevere? That's when you find out what your teammates are made of. That's when you get to see your own character, without the smoke screen of excuses.

If you've never competed in front of a crowd, how can you possibly know what it feels like to stand up in front of board members, or your company's senior management, or your own subordinate staff members, and explain how a project has crumbled? How can you find the reserves of courage and determination to pick yourself up from failure, analyze what went wrong, propose a new strategy, and win on the second try?

If you've never experienced it, this situation is going to feel utterly hopeless. But every athlete has been there.

You've been thumped. You've sat on the bench after a game, trying to hide your shame under a towel. You know that feeling.

But there's something else you know, too: it isn't the end of the world.

You know, from experience, that if you shrug off defeat, work harder, prepare better, adopt a tighter strategy, and come back more determined, you'll come out on top the next time.

Perfection over and over again would be great, but everybody knows perfection isn't infinitely sustainable. At some point, anything created by a human being is going to experience failure. It's when you're losing a game or your business plan just isn't bearing fruit that you show your character.

Whether it's in the competitive athletic arena or the give-and-take of the corporate environment, eventually you are going to find yourself in a fight-or-flight situation.

Think back to your own athletic days. No matter how naturally talented you were (an aerobic beast, a mass of fast-twitch muscles, born with the grace of a Nadia Comaneci, the power of a Serena Williams, and the tactics and vision of a Muhammad Ali) … no matter how incredible your coaches … no matter how lucky you were in your teammates— despite all that, there were times when you and your team were getting creamed.

What did you do when things got difficult?

Did you fold under pressure, throw in the towel, go through the motions with your eye on the game clock, wishing the misery would be over?

Or, did you persevere?

Did you struggle on through to the buzzer, maybe winning, maybe coming out on the short end of the stick, but whatever the outcome, able to walk off the court with your head held high?

We were playing in Russia, in a freezing cold arena, and at halftime, we were down by 30 points.

This had literally never happened to us before. We were training for the 1996 Olympics, we were undefeated in all our practice games, and here we were — losing to the Russians by 30 points.

They were so excited, because it really looked like they were going to beat the USA. They were ahead by 30 points, and nobody comes back from 30 points in the second half.

In fact, it might be that none of us on that team had ever, at any level of the sport, been behind by 30 points. We were being crushed. We didn't know how to respond.

Our coach gathered us together in the locker room. "Here's what we're going to do," she said.

I could see some of the players throwing glances at each other, and it was obvious they were thinking: What we're going to do is ... we're going to lose.

But the coach said, "Here's what we're going to do. First, we're going to play together; we're going to play like a team. And, second, we're going to break those 30 points down into smaller segments. Don't worry about 30 points. Let's go out there and pick up 10. Play solid defense, make sure they're one and done, box out as a team, rebound, and pick up 10 points."

"But we need 30," groaned one of the players.

"No," said the coach. "We need ten!"

The team leaders looked around at everyone. "Ten points is totally doable!"

So we ran back onto the court, focused on picking up 10 points, and within six minutes, we were behind by 20.

We gathered around the coach. "Do it again," she said, "Pick up 10 points."

Instead of throwing in the towel, we concentrated on those next 10 points. Suddenly, we were down by 10, and this was starting to look like familiar territory. One time or another, we'd all experienced coming back from a 10-point deficit. And no 10-point lead is ever safe against the USA.

You know the end of the story.

We broke that enormous deficit down into manageable chunks, we showed our true character, we persevered when times got tough, we played as a team, we didn't take any shortcuts, and we won.

When they are in that inevitable fight-or-flight situation, some people's natural response is to panic and flee.

But what a lot of us (you, too, we're betting) learned in our athletic days was that the productive response to fight-or-flight is to calm down and think through the problem, break it down into manageable tasks, and start getting them done, one after another.

In business, too, there will be situations in which you find yourself clouded with anger, frustration, or fear. That's only natural. Sometimes the stakes are really high, the chances for success look rather dim, and the consequences for failure are severe. Of course, your emotions are going to be gearing up.

We've all been there, lots of times.

But what we learned in sports is: Calm down, think through the problem, and *persevere.* Don't give up. Look at your challenges from another angle.

Back in the Blitz during World War II, the British government had a slogan: *Keep calm and carry on.*

It's a good one.

Don't lose your head. Don't give up hope. Just like you did when you were an athlete, keep doing what you know you need to do. Choose to persevere through the tough times, keep a level head, keep pushing forward, keep playing by the rules of the game, refuse to take any shortcuts, and learn from your mistakes.

I remember when one of the executives reporting to me in a large, service-based company wanted to add to his team and make a strategic hire. His top pick was a really smart guy with impressive presentation skills. I can see why he made it past the first round or two of interviews. However, given the specific requirements of this role and the missing "been there and done that" experience from the candidate, I knew he was absolutely the wrong person for the job. I knew that the moment I met him, but the young executive bucking to grow his team was convinced this would be an excellent hire.

I knew my young executive needed to learn through experience. How else would he learn to hire the right talent? I decided to make the investment and let it happen. So, the day my exec made the hire, I wrote him a note, sealed it, and dated it.

Six months later, when we fired the really smart guy who just wasn't a good fit, I gave my executive the sealed, dated envelope, and I told him, "This is not an "I told you so." This is an expression of how much I trust you. This is a demonstration of how important it is to me that you learn."

I consider the six months of salary we paid to have been an investment in my executive's professional education.

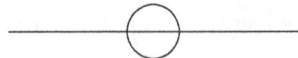

If you never learn to trust your subordinates, if you never learn to let them have their own chance to make a few mistakes and develop their skills, you'll be shooting yourself in the foot. If you haven't allowed anybody to prepare themselves to take your place ... if your lack of trust has made you irreplaceable ... then you can't be promoted — bad for your people, and bad for you, too.

We all have our heroes, those individuals in sports, business, politics, the arts, and other areas who have demonstrated perseverance, modeled courage, and shown us how to succeed within the rules. Here's one from more than 60 years ago: Roger Bannister.

In all the world of sports, there are a few catch phrases that everyone knows: a "perfect ten," the "career grand slam," and "the four-minute mile."

Throughout the 20th century, the world record in the one-mile run had been brought down little by little, and several athletes, notably Australian John Landy and Englishman Roger Bannister, were within seconds of breaking four minutes.

Bannister had shown talent from the first time he laced up a pair of running spikes, but as a committed medical student, he rarely had the time to train with the same intensity as his rivals. As a result, he had a checkered racing career: several British records, a few victories, a fourth place in the 1,500 meters in the 1952 Olympics, and losses to numerous competitors.

But Bannister eventually made the decision: he would be the man to crash through that monumental barrier. He would break the four-minute mile.

While spending incredibly long days as a physician-in-training, he designed for himself a specialized training regimen. He cut no corners. With Landy making several close-but-unsuccessful attempts at four minutes, Bannister persevered. And in June 1954, at the Iffley Road track in Oxford, Bannister pulled out all the stops. All alone, he sprinted the last lap. A photo of him collapsing across the finish line, utterly spent, would become famous worldwide. The announcer spoke through the public address system: *"Ladies and gentlemen, here is the result of event nine, the one mile: first, number forty one, R. G. Bannister, Amateur Athletic Association and formerly of Exeter and Merton Colleges, Oxford, with a time which is a new meeting and track record, and which—subject to ratification—will be a new English*

Native, British National, All-Comers, European, British Empire and World Record. The time was three ..." The crowd exploded in cheers, drowning out the rest of the time: 3:59.4.

Bannister's barrier-busting run is the story of a talented athlete who took no shortcuts, never lost sight of his goals, and despite setbacks along the way, *persevered.*

He showed what was possible, and within a few weeks, Landy followed Bannister and also ran the mile in under four minutes.

So, what's the point of remembering Bannister's achievement?

In the last few years, we've watched the major league home-run record being shattered in a thrilling year-long competition between two fantastic athletes, only to be horribly disappointed to learn that both of them appeared on a list of baseball players who used illegal performance- enhancing drugs.

We've witnessed the tainting of the Tour de France bicycle race by drug use.

In Bannister's own sport of track and field, we've seen shot putters, sprinters, and middle-distance runners caught using PEDs. World records set by doped athletes are so far beyond the limits of human capability (by legal athletes, anyway) that today's athletes don't even bother to try for them.

In the business world, we've seen Ponzi schemes steal millions of dollars from trusting investors. We've seen Enron collapse in the aftermath of corporate fraud and corruption. We've seen companies report fake earnings. We've seen companies misreport loans as sales. And so on and so on — it saddens us to acknowledge how widespread cutting corners is.

Wouldn't it be wonderful if we were able to admire our sports heroes and our business heroes, with absolutely no doubt that they had played within the rules? Wouldn't it be great to know their achievements were the result of talent and hard work?

In tough times, who are you?

Did you build a foundation of aggressive-but-fair play when you were a Little League ballplayer, a high school basketball player, or an age-group sprinter?

Have you carried that foundation into your business career?

We believe that we — all of us, including the authors and the readers of *From the Court to the Boardroom* — have it within us to be part of a cultural transformation.

Let's lead by example, succeeding through perseverance … playing the game aggressively, but within the rules … cutting no corners.

When the game is over, let's walk away with our heads held high, knowing we played hard, played to win, and played fair.

Chalk Talk
- Chapter 5 -

* REMOVE
  THE EMOTION

* SET AND ACHIEVE
  INCREMENTAL GOALS

* LEARN FROM YOUR
  FAILURES

Empower Through Leadership

The true goals of every leader are to build a team of leaders, to lead by way of influence, and, finally, to extend the reach of her leadership to an ever-widening community.

By demonstrating courage, intensity, ethics, and fairness, you identify yourself as the person to follow.

You become recognized as the person deserving of trust, the bastion of competency, the guru of strategy — in short, the leader.

You bring the group—whether it's your basketball teammates or your business colleagues — together into a cohesive unit that's running on all cylinders. By bringing them together, you make it possible to take advantage of—to amplify!—all the talents, skills, knowledge, intuition, insights, education, and abilities they possess.

You make it possible to turn your team, your office, your work unit, and your company into a winner!

When I arrived at the University of Southern California, despite the fact that I was just an 18-year-old freshman, I had very definite expectations for how my teammates were going to practice and play. I came in as the number one recruit in the nation, and I hadn't got to that position without thousands of hours of giving it my all in practice and games. I expected my new teammates to practice just as hard as I did. After all, the university they played for had a tradition of success to uphold.

Within just a few days, I was one disappointed freshman.

My teammates tended to practice their skills in a rather lackadaisical manner, with none of the crisp, attacking attitude they would need in a game.

Seniors cut corners in our running drills.

When our coach told us to make a certain number of layups, I saw them counting misses as makes, then taking a seat and chatting with each other about anything but basketball.

I looked around, expecting to hear someone say, "Hey, guys, this just isn't going to cut it. If we play games like we're practicing, we're going to get our butts kicked." But no one was stepping forward and assuming the mantle of team leader.

So I went to the coach and asked, "When can I start telling the other players what to do?"

She told me, "Before you can be vocal—before your teammates will be willing to listen to you—you are going to have to lead by example."

I took that to heart.

When we ran those suicide drills, the players on both sides of me might turn before they reached the line, but I made damn sure I ran all the way. When one player is running all the way, it's really obvious that the others are slacking off.

When we did layups, I concentrated, did my best to make every single one, and when I missed, I kept on doing the drill until I'd finished it to perfection. Everybody might be done (or as done as they planned to get), but there was the 18-year-old freshman, still finishing.

I didn't open my mouth to tell anyone what to do, but within days, there was a sea-change in everyone's attitude. Practices ran hard and sharp. Conditioning improved, skills improved, teamwork improved.

Well, that's great, I remember telling myself. Now when do I get to relax? Then I realized: Having made the choice to be a team leader meant that I never got to relax. I never got to take a day off, because my teammates were looking to me for leadership — every single day.

That's not an easy situation to be in. After all, most players, even the best, take an occasional day off, either skipping a workout or just giving themselves permission to take it easy today. But that's not an option for the leader. She needs to be on, every single day.

So, I decided to make consistency the hallmark of my style.

During practices, every one of my teammates knew what I was going to bring — every single day.

I showed up early for practice. All alone out there on the court, I would take hundreds of shots. Within a few days, one or two other players—inspired, I suppose, by a combination of shame and inspiration — were out there with me. Pretty soon, there were eight or nine of us. Eventually, it was the entire team. It became part of the culture of that team. As a group, we got better.

In games, I decided that I was responsible for a certain amount of production. If 20 points and 10 rebounds became my standard, then it was incredibly important to me that my teammates could count on that in every game. Sometimes I might end up with 25 or 30. That would be great! Sometimes I might have a little bit of an off-night, and I'd only score 15 or 17. But it was important to me that my teammates could count on me to score somewhere in that ballpark. Then, they could use my production as starting place and build their own games around that.

All of that, you'll notice, happened without opening my mouth and telling anyone what to do.

It was just what my coach sent me out to do: leadership by example.

It worked at USC, and we've seen it work in business, too. The successful business leader shows up — consistently. If I show you that I'm willing to run through a wall for you, on the basketball court or in the corporate world, then chances are, you'll consider running through a wall for me.

If you've made the decision to be a leader — because it *is* a choice— then what is it you are you deciding you want to achieve?

You've decided to empower, reward, encourage, and support. You've made the choice to inspire everyone to step it up a notch.

Ultimately, you've decided to build a team of leaders.

Not everyone is going to become the recognized leader of the team or the voice of the group — but every player has it in her to lead, in her own special way.

Let's assume you've absorbed the leadership lessons that athletics has to teach you. You're a team player, not a glory hog. You possess an honest joy in performing at the highest possible level. You've become a superb listener, hanging on every word your coach tells you.

At one time, you even considered becoming a coach. You thought being a leader like your coach seemed really rewarding.

You took those lessons with you into the classroom. At whatever level you've studied, you've always found a coach. That coach might have worn a professor's patch-elbow tweed and lacked a whistle around his neck, but he was a coach just the same.

Now, you've made it to your first big job, and one of the first things you do after you've settled into your upper-story corner office (well, okay, your cubicle … but you're prepared to be patient) is to look around for your coach. This is second nature to you by now. It's how your world has always worked.

Unfortunately, that isn't how the business world works.

In this new environment, you'll discover that no one is really going to be watching you until you do something so stellar that it attracts attention all up and down the hierarchy — or, until you do something equally terrible.

As a competitor, you've been accustomed to constant feedback, and now it just isn't there. But that doesn't mean you have no resources to depend on.

I will be forever grateful to a mentor who took me aside more than 15 years ago.

Though I didn't have the words for it at the time, she was giving back what had once been given to her. She was extending her positive reach, and I was the fortunate recipient.

I thought I was on a really great trajectory with the company I was working with at the time. I was on fire (or so I thought). I had won numerous awards and was lighting up scorecards.

Like most young and high-potential employees, I had become frustrated with what I perceived to be red tape and bad internal processes. Without being totally aware of it, I was letting it impact my day-to-day interactions with my colleagues and negatively affect my performance. I was becoming a distraction.

I was ready to tender my resignation. I had it typed up and was ready to hand it over, mistakenly (and painfully) believing that I was making such a difference; they would clear up these issues to keep me focused. This woman, Katherine, came to me and said, "Hey, you know what? You're really talented, but I think you're valuing your accomplishments higher than deserved. You are not doing the job you seem to think you are doing."

That put me back on my heels. You go through all kinds of emotions, none of them pleasant, when somebody tells you something like that. But it was absolutely necessary for me to hear that and face reality.

Then she did me an even bigger favor, sending me to what I still refer to as "charm school." Essentially, she sent me to a Leadership Development workshop that would help me explore the results of my first 360^0. If you have not had a 360^0, let me just tell you, it is an eye-opener. A 360^0 is an anonymous, honest portfolio of commentary and analysis of ... yep, you guessed it ... you.

Needless to say, sending me to this workshop didn't help much in the charm department, but it did some really incredible things for me. As I mentioned, the 360^0 was brutal—every executive, every coworker, people who reported to me, people who supervised me—she had all of them provide me honest, brutal, anonymous, 360-degree panoramic feedback on my attitude, my personality, my way of presenting myself, my skills, my performance, and the impact I was having on the organization.

I learned about some deficiencies that I hadn't recognized. I learned some things I needed to fix. It wasn't all bad, of course; I learned about some positive qualities that I hadn't thought were very important.

And one thing I really learned: I need a coach.

I believe that Leaders are Learners. Ever since that "charm school," I've known that learning must be a constant process, and I've sought out coaches and mentors to help me continually improve. Sometimes it's been a very formal process, and sometimes I've simply sat someone down and said, "Hey, I need to know what you think about my performance this past quarter."

If you are a mid- or late-career leader, or if you are an early-career person who sees himself or herself as a potential leader, bringing your best game, consistently and dependably, is essential. You need your teammates, colleagues, supervisors, and subordinates to know they can count on you to bring your best, every single day.

But to be a leader, at whatever level, is also to recognize that you have a responsibility to REACH: to mentor, to volunteer, to be of service. In one situation, mentoring might be inviting a teammate who's struggling to stay after practice to sharpen her shots. In another situation, it might mean one-on-one talks with a colleague, providing feedback on a project, or inviting the colleague to engage in a "360º charm school." Sometimes, it means simply sitting down with a colleague, lending an empathetic ear, listening to her concerns, and letting her know she isn't alone.

Being a mentor is a big job because you're not just addressing a skill set or helping someone change their competency: you're also helping them holistically grow as a person. It really is a full-on service job.

Texas A&M has a mentorship program for traditional MBA students, and I've signed up on the spot every year. These are the real go-getters. They have a million ideas, and they want to hear your feedback and advice on every single one of them. It's a lot like having another kid in your house. All of a sudden, you're taking all these calls.

Now I can't imagine not signing up, because even though I know it's going to be a lot of work, the alternative would be to just turn my head. It's become a lot like not voting — something I don't even need to think about.

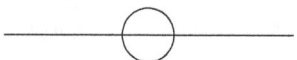

A leader isn't always on the lookout for some immediate reward, either.

We've seen a considerable number of successful businesspeople walk away at the end of their careers, thinking, "I've achieved everything by the sweat of my brow, and I've done plenty of one-on-one mentoring. I don't owe anything to some ambiguously defined community of future businesspeople, when I'm not even going to be around to reap the benefit." In our opinion, these guys have missed the chance to self-actualize themselves as true leaders. By refusing to take the opportunity to share their knowledge and experience with "the masses," we believe they've missed the chance to fully mature as leaders.

Whoever you are—a late-career, successful businessperson, a freshly minted MBA, or a current university student—you possess incredibly valuable experience and hard-won knowledge. We strongly encourage you to seek opportunities to share what you've learned in a volunteer capacity.

Sometimes, one woman will see another woman in need, and instead of reaching out to help her, the woman will sink her. It's unfortunate, but it's too often true. Instead of seeing the woman who's struggling as a colleague, someone to be helped, we view her as a competitor.

That's why I started "Life Support."

It's a women's group, designed to be a regular place where woman can meet and discuss questions that so many of us have, questions about life, relationships, and how to balance being a professional with being a wife and a mom. When we get together, we discover that we might put on a really strong façade in the workplace, but we are all dealing with the same issues. Instead of competing so hard against each other, we provide support, and everyone benefits.

But it's not only women who need support. One of my clients is a man who supports other men in becoming — to use his phrase — less transactional and more transformational in their leadership roles. He encourages them to focus a little bit less on being results-driven, to think about ways they can contribute to transforming the world.

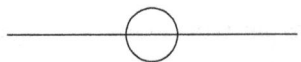

We encourage you to consider: *How can I return some value to my community? How can I give some other deserving young people a start on their upward climb?*

Consider what you can give back. We guarantee you'll benefit, too.

When I was in high school, Pete Newell was holding his annual Big Man's Camp at my high school.

Big Man's Camp is a summer camp for NBA post players, six feet nine and taller. Nearly all of them, from every team, take part in it. Some years, it's in Los Angeles, and some years, it's in Hawaii. For some reason, that year he'd scheduled it at Morningside High.

I wanted to be in the gym to see Pete teach the big men, so I volunteered to work the clock.

When they took breaks, I would grab a ball, get out there on the court, and try to mimic what I'd seen these NBA players doing.

Eventually Pete took notice, and he came over and ran me through several of the drills. Then he told me, "Tomorrow, I don't want you on the clock. I'll get somebody else to do that. I want you to get in line with the men."

What a dream that was! Me, a high school player, lining up with the best tall men in the NBA, running drills with them, learning moves from the best.

All because I volunteered to work the clock.

Sometimes your reward for volunteering is not so clear cut, but in all of our volunteer activities, we've never failed to come out ahead.

These days, our primary volunteer effort is something we call EmpoweredW, which evolved from our Leadership 2.0 initiative (*From the Court to the Boardroom* originated in Leadership 2.0, too).

EmpoweredW is an online community of women that we created as a way to "put our money where our mouth is." We launched it out of our hearts and out of our own pockets in order to help young female entrepreneurs, innovators, and thought leaders succeed through mentorship, guidance, and coaching. Our goal is to make EmpoweredW a place where established professional women — the two of us, but many others, too, as well as top universities — share best practices, content, insight, and networking experiences that enhance young women's early careers, nurture their emerging entrepreneurial mindset, and propel them into leadership roles.

We are personally involved in EmpoweredW, but we've designed it as a community centered around the "pay it forward" idea: a credit system ensures that the participant benefits while giving. If you're intrigued by the EmpoweredW concept — and we hope you are! — we encourage you to learn more about it, or even join, at http://empoweredw.com.

Chalk Talk
- Chapter 6 -

* BUILD A TEAM OF LEADERS

* LEAD VIA INFLUENCE

* THE DUTY OF LEADERSHIP

Our Wish for You

n the foreword to this book, our friend Magic Johnson made a brief list of the skills that all of us — Magic, Lisa, Bridgette, and you, too! — acquired in our playing days: leadership, determination, teamwork, and striving for excellence.

The point we've tried to make in the pages of this book is that those qualities, once learned on the playing field, the track, or the basketball court, are never lost. They remain embedded in our minds, in our personalities, and in our muscles, ready to be called up whenever they're needed.

You may not be consciously aware of possessing those qualities. You may not be actively using those skills.

You may think they were important for you as an athlete but don't have anything to do with you as a career person.

We disagree — strongly.

We learned those skills and acquired those qualities as young athletes. They served us well in our competitive days, and though we may have allowed them to drift to the back of our minds, they remain part of us, waiting to be called upon, revitalized, and applied to the challenges of our careers.

They are waiting, whenever we are ready, to re-ignite, rise, and reach.

As a brief reminder, here are the basic steps that have worked for us — and we're confident will work for you, too:

- We strive to lead by example.
- We aim to have the heart of a champion, leading us from good to great.
- We always try to display a winning attitude.
- We share the glory.
- We persevere, always (but especially in tough times) keeping in mind who we are.
- We seek to empower others through leadership.

By applying these steps in our careers, we've achieved a lot of success.

We believe success is waiting for you, too.

The lessons that made you a winner in your athletic years — we are absolutely convinced — make success achievable to you today.

Those lessons, called forth and applied to today's challenges, will make you a winner in your career, but as you were in sports.

That is what we sincerely wish for you — to be *a winner!*

Morgan James
Speakers Group

↗ www.TheMorganJamesSpeakersGroup.com

We connect Morgan James published
authors with live and online events
and audiences whom will benefit
from their expertise.

Morgan James makes all of our titles available
through the Library for All Charity Organization.

www.LibraryForAll.org

Printed in the USA
CPSIA information can be obtained
at www.ICGtesting.com
LVHW040341021023
759847LV00004B/505